TONY KUSHNER

Tony Kushner's first plays include *A Bright Room Called Day* and his adaptation of Corneille's *The Illusion*. His work has been ~oduced at the Mark Taper Forum, the New York Shakespeare stival, New York Theatre Workshop, Hartford Stage Company, rkeley Repertory Theatre and the Los Angeles Theatre Center, well as other theatres around the United States and abroad. He is e recipient of the 1990 Whiting Foundation Writers Award and ywriting and directing fellowships from the New York undation for the Arts, the New York State Council on the Arts d the National Endowment for the Arts. Tony Kushner was born Manhattan in 1956 and grew up in Lake Charles, Louisiana. lives in New York City.

gels in America, Parts One and Two, was commissioned by the reka Theatre company through a special projects grant from the tional Endowment for the Arts. The plays have been seen in San ancisco, at the Mark Taper Forum in Los Angeles, and in ydney, Australia. Part One, *Millennium Approaches*, ran for a ar in London at the Royal National Theatre. *Perestroika* opened ere, in repertory with a revival of *Millennium*, on 20 November 93. *Millennium* opened at the Walter Kerr Theatre on Broadway May 1993 and was joined by *Perestroika* on 23 November 93.

ngels has received two Fund for New American Plays/American xpress awards, the Los Angeles Drama Critics Circle Award for Best New Play of 1992 and the Outstanding Theatre Award from he Gay and Lesbian Alliance Against Defamation/Los Angeles. *Millennium* received the 1991 National Arts Club's Joseph Kesselring Award, the Bay Area Drama Critics Award for Best Play of 1991, the London *Evening Standard* Award for Best Play of 1992 and the London Drama Critics Circle Award for Best New Play, the 1993 Pulitzer Prize for Drama, the 1993 Tony award for Best Play, and the New York Drama Critics Circle and Drama Desk awards for Best Play.

A Selection of Other Volumes in this Series

*Published by Theatre Communications Group, distributed by Nick Hern Books

TONY KUSHNER

ANGELS IN AMERICA

A Gay Fantasia on National Themes

Part Two: Perestroika

ROYAL NATIONAL THEATRE
London

NICK HERN BOOKS
London

Angels in America Part Two: Perestroika
first published in Great Britain in 1994
as a paperback original
jointly by the Royal National Theatre, London,
and Nick Hern Books Limited,
14 Larden Road, London W3 7ST
Reprinted 1996, 1998

Front cover: collage by Michael Mayhew

Typeset by Country Setting, Woodchurch, Kent TN26 3TB
Printed in Great Britain by Athenæum Press Ltd,
Gateshead, Tyne & Wear

ISBN 1 85459 255 6

A CIP catalogue record for this book is available from
the British Library

Because the soul is progressive,
it never quite repeats itself,
but in every act attempts the production
of a new and fairer whole.

Ralph Waldo Emerson
'On Art'

Acknowledgements

I've been working on *Perestroika* since 1989. In the process I've accumulated many debts.

Abundant support, both financial and emotional, was provided by my parents, Bill and Sylvia Kushner and my aunt Martha Deutscher. My father has been terrifically helpful as *Perestroika* has come to completion.

My brother and sister, Eric and Lesley Kushner, have supported me both in my work and in the difficult process of coming out; without their love and enthusiasm writing this would never have been possible. The same is true for Mark Bronnenberg, to whom *Millennium Approaches* was dedicated.

Dot and Jerry Edelstien, and Marcia, Tony and Alex Cunha made homes away from home for me.

Jim Nicola of New York Theatre Workshop has encouraged and advised me all the way, and so has Rosemary Tischler of the New York Shakespeare Festival. Together they shed blood for the play, literally. They have won my purple heart.

Joyce Ketay, the Wonder-Agent, and her associate Carl Mullert, have been incredible friends and guardians. Michael Petshaft makes life seem manageable and has helped me keep sane.

Gordon Davidson has been the most open-hearted and -handed producer/shepherd any playwright could ever want, and the whole staff of the Taper has been sensational, fabulous, divine.

The National Theatre staff has also been immensely supportive; and I am particularly grateful to Richard Eyre and Giles Croft for believing in the play even in its scruffiest stages.

I am also indebted to Rocco Landesmann, Jack Viertel, Paul Libin, Margo Lion, Susan Gallin, Herb Alpert, Fred Zollo and the angelic hosts of brave and honourable producers who gambled on this outrageous experiment on Broadway.

The play has benefited from the dramaturgical work of Leon Katz, and K.C. Davis, as well as the directors and actors who have participated in its various workshops and productions. Stephen

Spinella, Joe Mantello and particularly Ellen McLaughlin have made invaluable suggestions on shaping and editing.

Sigrid Wurschmidt, actress extraordinaire and angel of light, remains with the play though she's left the world.

David Esbjornson, who directed the play in its first draft in San Francisco, and has listened to and commented on its stories ever since.

Tony Taccone made invaluable structuring suggestions during his work on the play in Los Angeles.

Declan Donellan and Nick Ormerod directed and designed the play at the National Theatre in London. Their early insights and responses have been challenging and helpful and have goaded me to keep trying to make the play better.

George C. Wolfe has been an inspiring and indefatigable collaborator on this final stage of shaping the script; he's been brilliantly insightful, respectful, and galvanizing. The last step was the hardest, and I wouldn't have managed it without him.

Oskar Eustis commissioned *Angels in America* and has been intimately involved in every stage of its development. Without his great intelligence, talent, friendship and determination, the project would have been neither begun nor completed. I began *Angels* as a conversation, real and imaginary, between Oskar and myself; that conversation has never stopped, and I hope never will.

A few months after I started work on *Perestroika* my mother died of cancer. She's a mighty presence in the play.

In the fifteen years of our friendship Kimberly T. Flynn has taught me much of what I now believe to be true about life: theory and practice. Her words and ideas are woven through the work, and our life together is its bedrock. *Perestroika* is for Kimberly. This is her play as much as it is mine.

Playwright's Notes

A Disclaimer. Roy M. Cohn, the character, is based on the late Roy M. Cohn (1927-1986), who was all too real; for the most part the acts attributed to the character Roy are to be found in the historical record. But this Roy is a work of dramatic fiction; his words are my invention, and liberties have been taken with his story. The real Roy died in August of 1986. For purposes of the play my Roy dies in February.

I want to acknowledge my indebtedness to Harold Bloom's reading of the Jacob story, which I first encountered in his introduction to Olivier Revault D'Allones's *Musical Variations on Jewish Thought*, in which Bloom translates the Hebrew word for 'blessing' as 'more life'. Bloom expands on his interpretation in *The Book of J*.

Yiddish translation was graciously provided by Joachim Neugroschel, and additionally by Jeffrey Salant.

Ian Kramer, Esq., provided essential information about the juridical mischief of the Reagan-era Federal bench. The court cases in Act IV Scene Eight are actual cases with some of the names and circumstances changed.

The Characters

THE ANGEL, *four divine emanations, Fluor, Phosphor, Lumen and Candle, manifest in One: The Continental Principality of America. She has magnificent grey steel wings.*

PRIOR WALTER, *Louis's abandoned boyfriend. Before discovering that he has AIDS, worked occasionally as a club designer or caterer, mostly lives modestly off a small trust fund.*

LOUIS IRONSON, *a word processor working for the Second Circuit Court of Appeals.*

JOSEPH PORTER PITT, *chief clerk for Justice Theodore Wilson of the Federal Court of Appeals, Second Circuit.*

HARPER AMATY PITT, *Joe's wife, an agoraphobic with a mild Valium addiction and a much stronger imagination.*

HANNAH PORTER PITT, *Joe's mother, formerly of Salt Lake City, now staying in Brooklyn. Lives off her deceased husband's army pension.*

BELIZE, *a former drag queen and former lover of Prior's. A registered nurse. Belize's name was originally Norman Arriaga; Belize is a drag name that stuck.*

ROY M. COHN, *a successful New York lawyer and unofficial power broker now facing disbarment, and dying of AIDS.*

Other Characters in Part Two

ALEKSII ANTEDILLUVIANOVICH PRELAPSARIANOV, *the World's Oldest Bolshevik, played by the actress playing Hannah.*

MR. LIES, *Harper's imaginary friend, a travel agent, who in style of dress and speech suggests a jazz musician; he always wears a large lapel badge emblazoned 'IOTA' (The International Order of Travel Agents). He is played by the actor playing Belize.*

HENRY, *Roy's doctor, played by the actress playing Hannah.*

ETHEL ROSENBERG, *played by the actress playing Hannah.*

EMILY, *a nurse, played by the actress playing the Angel.*

Mannequins in the Diorama Room of the Mormon Visitors' Centre:

> **THE MORMON FATHER,** *played by the actor playing Joe.*
>
> **CALEB,** *an offstage voice; the voice of the actor playing Belize.*
>
> **ORRIN,** *an offstage voice; the voice of the actress playing the Angel.*
>
> **THE MORMON MOTHER,** *played by the actress playing the Angel.*

The Continental Principalities, *inconceivably powerful Celestial Apparatchik/Bureaucrat-Angels of whom the Angel of America is a peer:*

 THE ANGEL EUROPA, *played by the actor playing Joe.*
 THE ANGEL AFRICANII, *played by the actress playing Harper.*
 THE ANGEL OCEANIA, *played by the actor playing Belize.*
 THE ANGEL ASIATICA, *played by the actress playing Hannah.*
 THE ANGEL AUSTRALIA, *played by the actor playing Louis.*
 THE ANGEL ANTARCTICA, *played by the actor playing Roy.*

RABBI ISIDOR CHEMELWITZ, *an orthodox Jewish rabbi, played by the actress playing Hannah.*

SARAH IRONSON, *Louis's dead grandma, who was interred by Rabbi Chemelwitz in Part One, Act One. She is played by the actor playing Louis.*

TAPED VOICE: *the voice that introduces Prelapsarianov in Act One Scene One and the Council of Principalities in Act Three Scene Five, and that speaks the welcome and narrative introduction in the diorama, should be that of the actress playing the Angel. These taped intros should sound alike: not parodic but beautiful and serious, the way the unseen Angel sounds in* Millennium.

A Note about the Staging

The play benefits from a pared-down style of presentation, with minimal scenery and scene shifts done rapidly (no blackouts!) employing the cast as well as stagehands – which makes for an actor-driven event, as this must be. The moments of magic – all of them – are to be fully realized, as bits of wonderful *theatrical* illusion – which means it's OK if the wires show, and maybe it's good that they do, but the magic should at the same time be thoroughly amazing.

It should also be said that *Millennium Approaches* and *Perestroika* are very different plays, and if one is producing them in repertory the difference should be reflected in their designs. *Perestroika* proceeds forward from the wreckage made by the Angel's traumatic entry at the end of *Millennium*. A membrane has broken; there is disarray and debris.

Perestroika is essentially a comedy, in that issues are resolved, mostly peaceably, growth takes place and loss is, to a certain degree, countenanced. But all this happens only through a terrific amount of struggle, and the stakes are high. The angel, the scenes in Heaven, Prior's prophet scenes are not lapses into some sort of elbow-in-the-ribs playing style. The angel is immensely august, serious and dangerously powerful *always*, and Prior is running for his life, sick, scared and alone. Every moment must be played for its reality, the terms always life and death; only then will the comedy emerge. There is also a danger in easy sentiment. Eschew sentiment! Particularly in the final act – metaphorical though it may at times be (or maybe not), the problems the characters face are finally among the hardest problems – how to let go of the past, how to change and lose with grace, how to keep going in the face of overwhelming suffering. It shouldn't be easy.

The Angel's Cough

The cough is one simple, dry, barking cough, not wracking emphysemic spasms. Ellen McLaughlin's cough was a variation on a cat hacking up a furball. It was sharp, simple and effectively non-human.

Flying

If you are mounting a production of the play, and you have an airborne angel, which is a good thing, be warned: it's incredibly hard to make the flying work. Add a week to tech time.

A Note about Cutting

The final version of *Millennium Approaches* was edited more closely than *Perestroika* has been. The text can be performed as is, or in a shorter version made by eliminating one or all three of the following passages:

Act Five Scene Five: In the council of Continental Principalities. The entire introduction to the scene can be eliminated, and the scene begin with the Angel of America saying 'Most August Fellow Principalities, Angels Most High: I regret my absence at this session, I was detained.' If this cut is made, the taped introduction should say 'All Seven Myriad Infinite Aggregate Angelic Entities in Attendance, May Their Glorious Names Be Praised Forever and Ever, Hallelujah' instead of 'Six of Seven, etc . . .' and the scene should begin with Prior and the Angel of America standing in the midst of the Principalities, rather than entering after the scene begins.

Act Five Scenes Six and Seven can be cut. Scene Seven can be played after Harper's final speech, before the Epilogue; if the scene *is* moved, Prior does not appear in it.

The elimination of these passages allows for a more streamlined final act; I feel that some of the fun and complexity of the play is lost as a result. The decision should be made according to the specific circumstances of each production.

The actors, directors and designers who have worked on the play transformed it. What follows is a list of the play's professional productions to date.

Perestroika was first performed as a staged reading in conjunction with the production of *Millennium Approaches* presented by The Eureka Theatre in San Francisco, May 1991. Both reading and production were directed by David Esbjornson. Sets were designed by Tom Kamm, costumes by Sandra Woodall, and lights by Jack Carpenter and Jim Cave. The cast was as follows:

THE ANGEL	Ellen McLaughlin
PRIOR WALTER	Stephen Spinella
LOUIS IRONSON	Michael Ornstein
JOE PITT	Michael Scott Ryan
HARPER PITT	Anne Darragh
HANNAH PITT	Kathleen Chalfant
BELIZE	Harry Waters Jr.
ROY COHN	Jon Bellucci

The play was further developed in workshop and presented as a stage reading at the Mark Taper Forum in Los Angeles, May 1992. The workshop and reading were directed by Oskar Eustis and Tony Taccone. The cast was as follows:

THE ANGEL	Ellen McLaughlin
PRIOR WALTER	Stephen Spinella
LOUIS IRONSON	Joe Mantello
JOE PITT	Jeffrey King
HARPER PITT	Cynthia Mace
HANNAH PITT	Kathleen Chalfant
BELIZE	Harry Waters Jr.
ROY COHN	Larry Pressman

The World Premiere of *Perestroika* was presented by The Mark Taper Forum, in November 1992, directed by Oskar Eustis and Tony Taccone, with sets designed by John Conklin, lights by Pat Collins, costumes by Gabrielle Berry, and music by Mel Marvin. The cast was as follows:

THE ANGEL	Ellen McLaughlin
PRIOR WALTER	Stephen Spinella
LOUIS IRONSON	Joe Mantello
JOE PITT	Jeffrey King
HARPER PITT	Cynthia Mace
HANNAH PITT	Kathleen Chalfant
BELIZE	K. Todd Freeman
ROY COHN	Ron Leibman

The play was presented by New York University/Tisch School of the Arts, April 1993. It was directed by Michael Mayer, with sets by Tony Cisek and Andrew Hall, lights by Jack Mehler, costumes by Robin J. Orloff and music by Michael Ward. The cast was as follows:

THE ANGEL	Jenna Stern
PRIOR WALTER	Daniel Zelman
LOUIS IRONSON	Johnny Garcia
JOE PITT	Robert Carin
HARPER PITT	Debra Messing
HANNAH PITT	Vivienne Benesch
BELIZE	Mark Douglas
ROY COHN	Ben Schenkman

Perestroika opened in New York at the Walter Kerr Theatre on November 23, 1993, in a production directed by George C. Wolfe with sets by Robin Wagner, lights by Jules Fisher, costumes by Toni-Leslie James and music by Anthony Davis. The cast was as follows:

THE ANGEL	Ellen McLaughlin
PRIOR WALTER	Stephen Spinella
LOUIS IRONSON	Joe Mantello
JOE PITT	David Marshall Grant
HARPER PITT	Marci Gay Harden
HANNAH PITT	Kathleen Chalfant
BELIZE	Jeffrey Wright
ROY COHN	Ron Leibman

Angels in America Part Two: Perestroika was first performed in London on the Cottesloe stage of the National Theatre. First preview was 12 November and press night 20 November 1993. The cast, in order of speaking, was:

PRELAPSARIANOV	Harry Towb
THE ANGEL	Nancy Crane
PRIOR WALTER	Stephen Dillane
LOUIS IRONSON	Jason Isaacs
JOSEPH PORTER PITT	Daniel Craig
HARPER AMATY PITT	Clare Holman
MR LIES	Joseph Mydell
HANNAH PORTER PITT	Susan Engel
BELIZE	Joseph Mydell
HENRY, *Roy's Doctor*	Harry Towb
ROY M. COHN	David Schofield
EMILY, *Prior's Nurse*	Nancy Crane
ETHEL ROSENBERG	Susan Engel
VOICE AT MORMON VISITORS' CENTRE	Nancy Crane
MORMON FATHER	Daniel Craig
MORMON MOTHER	Nancy Crane
CALEB	Joseph Mydell
ORRIN	Nancy Crane
THE ANGELS	
AUSTRALIA	Jason Isaacs
EUROPA	Daniel Craig
AFRICANII	Clare Holman
ASIATICA	Susan Engel
OCEANIA	Joseph Mydell
SARAH IRONSON	Jason Isaacs
RABBI ISIDOR CHEMELWITZ	Harry Towb
RECORDED NEWSREADER	Robin Houston

Musicians
Duncan Chave *(keyboard)*, David Roach *(saxophone)*

Director	Declan Donnellan
Designer	Nick Ormerod
Lighting	Mick Hughes
Music	Paddy Cunneen
Director of Movement	Jane Gibson
Dialect Coach	Joan Washington
Company Voice Work	Patsy Rodenburg

ACT ONE: Spooj   January 1986

Scene One

In the darkness a Voice announces:

VOICE. In the Hall of Deputies, The Kremlin. January 1986.
Aleksii Antedilluvianovich Prelapsarianov, the World's Oldest
Living Bolshevik.

Lights up on PRELAPSARIANOV *at a podium before a great
red flag. He is unimaginably old and totally blind.*

ALEKSII ANTEDILLUVIANOVICH PRELAPSARIANOV. The
Great Question before us is: Are we doomed? The Great
Question before us is: Will the Past release us? The Great
Question before us is: Can we Change? In Time? And we all
desire that Change will come.

Little pause.

(With sudden, violent passion.) And Theory? How are we to
proceed without Theory? What System of Thought have these
Reformers to present to this mad swirling planetary
disorganization, to the Inevident Welter of fact, event,
phenomenon, calamity? Do they have, as we did, a beautiful
Theory, as bold, as Grand, as comprehensive a construct . . . ?
You can't imagine, when we first read the Classic Texts, when
in the dark vexed night of our ignorance and terror the seed-
words sprouted and shoved incomprehension aside, when the
incredible bloody vegetable struggle up and through into Red
Blooming gave us Praxis, True Praxis, True Theory married to
Actual Life . . . You who live in this Sour Little Age cannot
imagine the grandeur of the prospect we gazed upon: like
standing atop the highest peak in the mighty Caucasus, and
viewing in one all-knowing glance the mountainous, granite
order of creation. You cannot imagine it. I weep for you.
    And what have you to offer now, children of this Theory?
What have you to offer in its place? Market Incentives?
American Cheeseburgers? Watered-down Bukharinite stopgap
makeshift Capitalism! NEPmen! Pygmy children of a gigantic
race!
    Change? Yes, we must must change, only show me the
Theory, and I will be at the barricades, show me the book of the
next Beautiful Theory, and I promise you these blind eyes will
see again, just to read it, to devour that text. Show me the words

that will reorder the world, or else keep silent.

If the snake sheds his skin before a new skin is ready, naked he will be in the world, prey to the forces of chaos. Without his skin he will be dismantled, lose coherence and die. Have you, my little serpents, a new skin?

A tremendous tearing and crashing sound, the great red flag is flown out, and lights come up on the same tableau as at the close of Millennium Approaches: PRIOR *cowering in his bed, which is strewn with the wreckage of his bedroom ceiling; and the* ANGEL, *in a gown of surpassing whiteness, barefoot and magnificent, hovering in the air, facing him.*

ALEKSII ANTEDILLUVIANOVICH PRELAPSARIANOV.
Then we dare not we *cannot*, we MUST NOT move ahead!

ANGEL. Greetings, Prophet.
The Great Work Begins.
The Messenger has arrived.

PRIOR. Go away.

Scene Two

The same night as at the end of Millennium, *late.* JOE *and* LOUIS *at* LOUIS's *new apartment in the Arctic wastes of Alphabetland – barren of furniture, unpainted, messy, grim. Tense little pause.* LOUIS *embarrassed takes in the room.*

LOUIS. Alphabetland. This is where the Jews lived when they first arrived. And now, a hundred years later, the place to which their more seriously fucked-up grandchildren repair. (*Yiddish accent.*) This is progress?
    It's a terrible mess.

JOE. It's a little dirty.

LOUIS. *Messy*, not dirty . That's an important distinction. It's dust, not dirt, chemical-slash-mineral, not organic, not like microbes, more like . . . Can I take your tie off?

    LOUIS *reaches towards* JOE.

JOE (*stepping back*). No, wait, I'm, um, um, uncomfortable, actually.

LOUIS. Me too, actually. Being uncomfortable turns me on.

JOE. Your, uh, boyfriend.
    He's sick.

LOUIS. Very. He's not my boyfriend, we . . . We can cap everything that leaks in latex, we can smear our bodies with nonoxynol-9, safe, chemical sex. Messy, but not dirty.

Little pause.

Look I want to but I don't want to beg.

JOE. No, I . . .

LOUIS. Oh come on. *Please.*

JOE. I should go.

LOUIS. Fine! Oblahdee, oblahdah, life goes on. Rah.

JOE. What?

LOUIS. Hurry home to the missus.

(*Pointing to* JOE's *left hand*). Married gentlemen before cruising the Ramble should first remove their bands of gold.
   Go if you're going. Go.

JOE *starts to leave. There is a moment at the door,* JOE *hesitating,* LOUIS *watching him.* JOE *goes to* LOUIS, *hugs him.*

JOE. I'm not staying.

LOUIS (*sniffing*). What kind of cologne is that?

JOE. (*a beat, then*). Fabergé.

LOUIS. OH! *Very* butch, very heterosexual high school. Fabergé.

LOUIS *gently breaks the hug, steps back.*

You smell nice.

JOE. So do you.

LOUIS. Smell is . . . an incredibly complex and underappreciated physical phenomenon. Inextricably bound up with sex.

JOE. I . . . didn't know that,

LOUIS. It is. The nose is really a sexual organ.
   Smelling. Is desiring. We have five senses, but only two that go beyond the boundaries . . . of ourselves. When you look at someone, it's just bouncing light, or when you hear them, it's just sound waves, vibrating air, or touch is just nerve-endings tingling. Know what a smell is?

JOE. It's . . . some sort of . . . No.

LOUIS. It's made of the molecules of what you're smelling. Some part of you, where you meet the air, is airborne. (*He goes up to* JOE, *close*.) Little molecules of Joe . . . (*He inhales deeply*.)

Up my nose. Mmmm . . . Nice. Try it.

JOE. Try . . . ?

LOUIS. Inhale.

JOE inhales.

LOUIS. Nice?

JOE. Yes.

I . . .

LOUIS (*quietly*). Ssssshhhh.

Smelling. And tasting. First the nose, then the tongue.

JOE. I just don't . . .

LOUIS. They work as a team, see. The nose tells the body – the heart, the mind, the fingers the cock – what it wants, and then tho tongue explores, finding out what's edible, what isn't, what's most mineral, food for the blood, food for the bones, and therefore most delectable.

He licks the side of JOE's cheek.

Salt.

LOUIS *kisses JOE, who holds back a moment and then responds.*

Mmm. Iron. Clay.

LOUIS *slips his hand down the front of JOE's pants. They embrace more tightly. LOUIS pulls his hand out, smells and tastes his fingers, and then holds them for JOE to smell.*

LOUIS. Chlorine. Copper. Earth.

They kiss again.

LOUIS. What does that taste like?

JOE. Um . . .

LOUIS. What?

JOE. Well . . . Nighttime.

LOUIS. Stay?

JOE. Yes.

Still stalling:

Louis?

LOUIS (*unbuttoning JOE's shirt*). Hmmm?

JOE. What did that mean, oblahdee oblah . . .

LOUIS. Sssssh. Words are the worst things. Breathe. Smell.

JOE. But . . .

LOUIS. Let's stop talking. Or if you have to talk, talk dirty.

Scene Three

MR. LIES *is sitting alone playing the oboe, in* HARPER'*s imaginary Antarctica.* HARPER *enters dragging a small pine tree which she has felled. The fantasy explorer gear is gone; she is dressed in the hastily-assembled outfit in which she fled the apartment at the end of Act Two of* Millennium*; she's been outdoors for three days now and looks it – filthy and dishevelled.*

HARPER. I'm FREEZING! IT IS TOO COLD! What happened to global warming?

MR. LIES (*stops playing, pointing to the tree*). Where did you get that?

HARPER. Um . . . From the . . . the great Antarctic pine forests. Right over that hill.

MR. LIES. There are no pine forests in Antarctica.

HARPER.This one's a blue spruce.

MR. LIES. You keep messing with the idyllic, you're gonna wind up to your knees in slush.

HARPER. I chewed this pine tree down. With my teeth. Like a beaver. I'm *hungry*, I haven't eaten in three days! I'm going to use it to build . . . something, maybe a fire.

MR. LIES *resumes his oboe playing. For a moment, the magical Antarctic light begins to dim, replaced by the glare of sodium park lights; the sea-sounds and wind are drowned out by the sound of traffic as heard from the middle of a city park at night; Harper looks about, and as she does Antarctica is restored a bit, though the city lights and sounds do not retreat entirely.*

MR. LIES. The oboe: official instrument of the International Order of Travel Agents. If the duck was a songbird it would sing like this. Nasal, desolate, the call of migratory things.

JOE *enters the scene, looking around, uncertain of where he is till he sees* HARPER. *He has* LOUIS'*s bedsheet wrapped around his waist.*

MR. LIES. The Eskimo is back.

HARPER. I know.

I wanted a real Eskimo, one with sense enough to put on pants in sub-zero weather, not this, this is just . . .

JOE. Hey, buddy.

HARPER. I don't understand why I'm not dead. When your heart breaks, you should die.

But there's still the rest of you. There's your breasts, and your genitals, and they're amazingly stupid, like babies or faithful dogs, they don't get it, they just want him. Want him.

JOE. I looked for you. I've been everywhere.

HARPER. Like that? It's indecent.

JOE. No, I . . . I'm not looking now. I guess I'm having an adventure.

HARPER. Is it . . . fun?

JOE. Scary fun. Yes.

HARPER. Can I come with you? This isn't working anymore. I'm cold.

JOE. I wouldn't want you to see.

HARPER. Think it's worse than what I imagine? It's not.

JOE. I should go.

HARPER. Bastard. You fell out of love with me.

JOE. That isn't true, Harper.

HARPER. Then come back.

Little pause.

JOE. I can't.

He vanishes. MR. LIES *plays the oboe, a brief, wild lament. The magic Antarctic night is now completely gone. The ordinary sounds of the park and the city in the distance.*

MR. LIES. Blues for the death of heaven.

HARPER. If I was a good Mormon I could have pulled it off.

MR. LIES. You overreached. Tore a big old hole in the sky. No Eskimo in Antarctica.

HARPER. No. No trees either.

MR. LIES (*pointing to the chewed-down pine tree*). So where did you get that?

HARPER. From the Botanical Gardens Arboretum. It's right over
    there. Prospect Park. We're still in Brooklyn I guess.

The lights of a police car begin to flash.

MR. LIES (*vanishing*). The Law for real.

HARPER (*raising her arms over her head*). Busted. Damn.
    What a lousy vacation.

Scene Four

*In the Pitt apartment in Brooklyn. A telephone rings. HANNAH,
carrying the bags she had with her and wearing the coat she had
in Act Three Scene Four of* Millennium, *enters the apartment,
drops the bags, runs for the phone.*

HANNAH. Pitt residence.
    No, he's out. No I have no idea where he is. I have no idea.
I have no idea. No idea. No. No. This is his mother. OH MY
LORD! Is she . . . You . . . Wait, officer, I don't . . . You found
her in the . . . Prospect Park? I don't . . . She *what*? A pine tree?
Why on earth would she chew a . . .
    (*Very severe.*) Well you have no business laughing about it,
so you can stop that right now, that's ugly.
    I don't know where that is, I just arrived from Salt Lake and
I barely found Brooklyn. I'll take a . . . a taxicab. Well yes of
course right now! *No.* No hospital. We don't need any of that.
She's not insane, she's just . . . peculiar. Tell her to behave. Tell
her . . . Mother Pitt is coming. (*She hangs up.*)

Scene Five

PRIOR *in bed, alone, asleep, later the same night. The room is
intact, no trace of the demolished ceiling. He is having a
nightmare. He wakes up.*

PRIOR. OH! Oh.

*He looks under the covers. He discovers that the lap of his
pyjamas is soaked in cum.*

Fuck fuck fuck.

Will you look at this! First goddam orgasm in months and I slept through it.

He picks up the telephone receiver, dials a number. The phone rings by BELIZE's workstation on the tenth floor of New York Hospital. BELIZE answers.

BELIZE. Ten East.

PRIOR. I am drenched in spooj.

BELIZE. Spooj?

PRIOR. Cum. Jiz. Ejaculate.

BELIZE. Spooj?

PRIOR. Onomatapoetic. isn't it.
I've had a wet dream.

BELIZE. Well about time. Miss Thing has been abstemious. She has stored up beaucoup de spooj.

PRIOR. It was a woman.

BELIZE. You turning straight on me?

PRIOR. Not a *conventional* woman.

BELIZE. Grace Jones?

Little pause. PRIOR looks at the ceiling.

BELIZE. Hello?

PRIOR. An angel.

BELIZE. Oh FABULOUS.

PRIOR. I feel . . . lascivious. Come over.

BELIZE. I spent the whole day with you, I *do* have a life of my own, you know.

PRIOR. I'm sad.

BELIZE. I thought you were lascivious.

PRIOR. Lascivious sad. Wonderful and horrible all at once, like . . . like there's a war inside. My eyes are funny, I . . .
(*He touches his eyes.*) Oh.
I'm crying.

BELIZE. Prior?

PRIOR. I'm scared. And also full of . . . I don't know, Joy or something. Hope.

In the hospital, HENRY, ROY's doctor, enters.

HENRY. Are you the duty nurse?

BELIZE. Yo .
>Look, baby, I have to go, I'll . . .

HENRY. Are you the duty nurse?

BELIZE (*to* HENRY). *Yo*, I said.

PRIOR. Sing something first. Sing with me.

HENRY. Why are you dressed like that?

BELIZE. You don't like it?

PRIOR. Just one little song. Some hymn.

HENRY. Nurses are supposed to wear white.

BELIZE. Doctors are supposed to be home, in Westchester, asleep.

>(*To* PRIOR.) What hymn?

PRIOR. Ummm . . . 'Hark the Herald Angels . . . '

HENRY. *Nurse.*

BELIZE (*to* HENRY). One moment, *please*. This is an emergency.

>(*To* PRIOR, *singing*.) Hark the Herald Angels sing.

PRIOR (*joining in*). Glory to the newborn king.
>Peace on earth and mercy mild,
>God and sinners reconciled . . .

HENRY (*over the song*). What's your name?

>BELIZE *sings louder*.

BELIZE and PRIOR.
>JOYFUL all ye nations rise,
>Join the triumph of the skies!
>With Angelic Hosts proclaim:
>Christ is born in Bethlehem!
>Hark the herald angels sing,
>Glory to the newborn king!

BELIZE. Call you back. There's a man bothering me.

PRIOR. Je t'aime.

>BELIZE *hangs up*.

BELIZE. Now may I help you doctor or are you just cruising me?

HENRY. Emergency admit, Room 1013. Here are the charts. (*He hands medical charts to* BELIZE.) Start the drip, Gamma G and he'll need a CTM, radiation in the morning so clear diet and . . .

BELIZE (*reading the chart*). 'Liver cancer'? Oncology's on six, doll.

HENRY. This is the right floor.

BELIZE. It says Liver cancer.

HENRY (*lashing out*). I don't give a *fuck* what it *says*. *I* said this is the right floor. Got it?

BELIZE. Ooooh, testy . . .

HENRY. He's a very important man.

BELIZE. Oh, OK. Then I *shouldn't* fuck up his medication?

HENRY. I'll be back in the morning.

BELIZE. Safe home.

   HENRY *leaves.*

BELIZE. Asshole.

   BELIZE *picks up phone, dials; PRIOR answers.*

BELIZE. I have some piping hot dish.

PRIOR. How hot can it be at three in the . . . ?

BELIZE. Get out your oven mitts.
      Guess who just checked in with the troubles?
      The Killer Queen Herself. New York's number one closeted queer.

PRIOR. *Koch?*

BELIZE. NO! Not Koch. (*He whispers into the receiver.*)

PRIOR (*shock, then*). The Lord moves in mysterious ways.

BELIZE. Fetch me the hammer and the pointy stake, girl. I'm a-going in.

Scene Six

ROY *in his hospital bed, sick and very scared.* BELIZE *enters with the IV drip.*

ROY. Get outa here you, I got nothing to say to you . . .

BELIZE. Just doing my . . .

ROY. I want a white nurse. My constitutional right.

BELIZE. You're in a hospital, you don't have any constitutional rights.

   He begins preparing ROY's right arm for the IV drip,

palpating the vein, disinfecting the skin etc.

ROY (*getting nervous about the needle*). Find the vein, you moron, don't start jabbing that goddammed spigot in my arm till you find the fucking vein or I'll sue you so bad they'll repossess your teeth you dim black motherf . . .

BELIZE (*had enough; very fierce*). Watch. Yourself.
You don't talk that way to me when I'm holding something this sharp. Or I might slip and stick it in your heart. If you have a heart.

ROY. Oh I do. Tough little muscle. Never bleeds.

BELIZE. I'll bet.
Now I've been doing drips a long time. I can slip this in so easy you'll think you were born with it. Or I can make it feel like I just hooked you up to a bag of liquid Drano. So you be nice to me or you're going to be one sorry asshole come morning.

ROY. Nice.

BELIZE. Nice and quiet.

BELIZE *puts the drip needle in* ROY's *arm.*

BELIZE. There.

ROY (*fierce*). I *hurt*.

BELIZE. I'll get you a painkiller.

ROY. Will it knock me out?

BELIZE. I sure hope so.

ROY. Then shove it. Pain's . . . nothing, pain's life.

BELIZE. Sing it, baby.

ROY. When they did my facelifts, I made the anaesthesiologist use a local. They lifted up my whole face like a dinner napkin and I was wide awake to see it.

BELIZE. Bullshit. No doctor would agree to do that.

ROY. I can get anyone to do anything I want. For instance:
Let's be friends. (*Sings.*) 'We shall overcome . . . '
Jews and Coloureds, historical liberal coalition, right? My people being the first to sell retail to your people, your people being the first people my people could afford to hire to sweep out the store Saturday mornings, and then we all held hands and rode the bus to Selma. Not me of course, I don't ride buses, I take cabs. But the thing about The American Negro is, he never went Communist. Loser Jews did. But you people had Jesus so the reds never got to you. I admire that.

BELIZE. Your chart didn't mention that you're delusional.

ROY. Barking mad. Sit. Talk.

BELIZE. Mr. Cohn. I'd rather suck the pus out of an abscess. I'd rather drink a subway toilet. I'd rather chew off my tongue and spit it in your leathery face. So thanks for the offer of conversation, but I'd rather not.

BELIZE starts to exit, turning off the light as he does.

ROY. Oh for christsake. Whatta I gotta do? Beg? I don't want to be alone.

BELIZE stops.

ROY. Oh how I fucking *hate* hospitals, nurses, this waste of time and . . . *wasting* and weakness, I want to kill the . . .
    'Course they can't kill this, can they?

Pause. BELIZE says nothing.

ROY. No. It's too simple. It knows itself. It's harder to kill something if it knows what it is.
    Like pubic lice. You ever have pubic lice?

BELIZE. That is none of your . . .

ROY. I got some kind of super crabs from some kid once, it took twenty drenchings of Kwell and finally shaving to get rid of the little bastards. *Nothing* could kill them. And every time I had to itch I'd smile, because I learned to respect them, these unkillable crabs, because . . . I learned to identify. You know? Determined lowlife. Like me.
    You've seen lots of guys with this . . .

BELIZE (*little pause, then*). Lots.

ROY. How do I look, comparatively?

BELIZE. I'd say you're in trouble.

ROY. I'm going to die. Soon.
    That was a question.

BELIZE. Probably. Probably so.

ROY. Hah.
    I appreciate the . . . the honesty, or whatever . . .
    If I live I could sue you for emotional distress, the whole hospital, but . . .
    I'm not prejudiced, I'm not a prejudiced man.

Pause. BELIZE just looks at him.

ROY. These racist guys, simpletons, I never had any use for them – too rigid. You want to keep your eye on where the most powerful enemy really is. I save my hate for what counts.

BELIZE. Well. And I think that's a good idea, a good thing to do, probably.

Little pause.

(*With great effort and distaste.*) This didn't come from me and I *don't* like you but let me tell you a thing or two:
    They have you down for radiation tomorrow for the sarcoma lesions, and you don't want to let them do that, because radiation will kill the T-cells and you don't have any you can afford to lose. So tell the doctor no thanks for the radiation. He won't want to listen. Persuade him.
    Or he'll kill you.

ROY. You're just a fucking nurse. Why should I listen to you over my very qualified, very expensive WASP doctor?

BELIZE. He's not queer. I am. (*He winks at* ROY.)

ROY. Don't wink at me.
    You said a thing or two. So that's one.

BELIZE. I don't know what strings you pulled to get in on the azidothymidine trials.

ROY. I have my little ways.

BELIZE. Uh-huh.
    Watch out for the double blind. They'll want you to sign something that says they can give you M&M's instead of the real drug. You'll die, but they'll get the kind of statistics they can publish in the *New England Journal of Medicine*. And you can't sue 'cause you signed. And if you don't sign, no pills.
    So if you have any strings left, pull them, because everyone's put through the double blind and with this, time's against you, you can't fuck around with placebos.

ROY. You hate me.

BELIZE. Yes.

ROY. Why are you telling me this?

BELIZE. I wish I knew.

Pause.

ROY (*very nasty*). You're a butterfingers spook faggot nurse.
    I think . . . you have little reason to want to help me.

BELIZE. Consider it solidarity. One faggot to another.

BELIZE *snaps, turns, exits.* ROY *calls after him.*

ROY. Any more of your lip, boy, and you'll be flipping Big Macs in East Hell before tomorrow night!

A beat. He picks up his bedside phone.

And get me a real phone, with a hold button, I mean look at this, it's just one little line, now how am I supposed to perform basic bodily functions on *this*?

He thinks a minute, picks up the receiver, clicks the hang-up button several times.

Yeah who is this, the operator? Give me an outside line. Well then dial for me. It's a medical emergency darling, dial the fucking number or I'll strangle myself with the phone cord. 202-733-8525.

Little pause.

Martin Heller. Oh Hi Martin. Yeah I know what time it is, I couldn't sleep, I'm busy dying. Listen Martin, this drug they got me on, azido-methatalo-molamoca-whatchamacallit. Yeah. AZT.

I want my own private stash, Martin. Of serious Honest-Abe medicine. That I control, here in the room with me. No placebos, I'm no good at tests, Martin, I'd rather cheat. So send me my pills with a get-well bouquet, *PRONTO*, or I'll ring up CBS and sing Mike Wallace a song: the ballad of adorable Ollie North and his secret contra slush fund.

He holds the phone away from his ear; Martin is excited.

Oh you only *think* you know all I know. *I* don't even know what all I know. Half the time I just make it up, and it *still* turns out to be true! We learned that trick in the fifties. Tomorrow, you two-bit scumsucking shitheel flypaper insignificant dried-out little turd. A nice big box of drugs for Uncle Roy. Or there'll be seven different kinds of hell to pay.

He slams the receiver down.

Scene Seven

The same night and then several nights after, over the course of three weeks. Split Scene: JOE and LOUIS in bed in Alphabetland. HANNAH and HARPER in the Pitt apartment in Brooklyn. HANNAH stands looking at HARPER, who is dressed in a nightdress, picking her teeth.

HANNAH. It's late now, you should get into bed.
    I can't believe you chewed down that tree.

HARPER. I thought I was a beaver. After that, the rest was easy.

HANNAH. Park trees are public property, Harper, you can't go around gnawing on . . .

HARPER (*glares at her, then*). This is Brooklyn, Mother Pitt. You live in Salt Lake. What are you doing here?

HANNAH. I sold my house.

> HARPER *turns around, goes back inside the bedroom, shutting the door.*

Can I get you some . . . tea, or . . . dental floss, or . . .

LOUIS. That was great. You were great. Was I? Great? Or good, even?

JOE. Sssshhh, no talk now, I just want to breathe.

LOUIS. OK.

> *Tense little pause.*

Why did you follow me tonight?

JOE (*a look at Louis, then*). I'm . . . suspended.
> Sort of remote from the earth. Like I've left no traces, like I haven't been here at all.

LOUIS. But . . .

JOE. Till tonight.
> I was here. With you. This has consequence. This was new.
> I keep expecting divine retribution for this, but . . .
> I'm . . . actually happy. Actually.

LOUIS. Are you . . . What? Catholic, or . . .

JOE. Um, Protestant. Sort of.

LOUIS. I don't believe in God. I think you should know
> that before we fuck again. I used to believe but . . . If there
> was a God He would've clobbered me by now. I'm the
> incontrovertible argument against the existence of a just
> God, or at least against His competence or attentiveness or . . .

JOE. Stop suffering.

LOUIS. I have no right not to suffer, if I failed to suffer the universe would become unbalanced.

> JOE *bites one of* LOUIS's *nipples.*

> HANNAH *enters the apartment dressed for work at the Mormon Visitors' Centre.* HARPER *is slouched in a chair.*

HANNAH. I'm back.

LOUIS. Oh God, Oh God, I *believe*, I *believe*!

JOE *and* LOUIS *begin to fuck again.*

HANNAH. You haven't been out of that nightdress in two weeks now.

HARPER (*dull, flat*). I watched TV before you got home.

HANNAH. Well that's progress.

HARPER. It was a show about Antarctica. Female polar bears were being chased by men in snowsuits. The men in snowsuits videotaped the polar bears running to escape. The bears went: (*She makes the deep wheezy hooting of a panicky animal.*) And their tongues lolled and their eyes rolled in their stupid tiny heads and the men stabbed them in their huge butts with hypodermic needles, knocked them out. And then they shoved frozen polar bear sperm-pencils up their cooters. The bears looked like rugs. The men all looked like . . .
    Good night.

HANNAH. There are no polar bears in Antarctica.

HARPER. THE ARCTIC THEN THE GODDAMNED ARCTIC WHAT THE FUCK DIFFERENCE DOES IT . . .

HANNAH. Profanity is *not* required.
    Dress yourself and come with me to the Visitors' Centre. Do some work.

HARPER. I don't want to work.

HANNAH. What do you want to do.

HARPER (*bright smile*). Die. (*She goes inside, slams the door.*)

Days pass. JOE *and* LOUIS, *still in bed.*

JOE. You think happiness is about being totally happy.

HANNAH. Are you going to stay in bed forever?

JOE. Since you believe the world is perfectable you find it always unsatisfying. But you must reconcile yourself to its unperfectability by being thoroughly *in* the world but not *of* it.

LOUIS. Sounds like schizophrenia.

JOE. No, it's the end of a nineteenth-century socialist romanticist conflation of government and society, law and Justice, idea and action, irreconcilables which only meet at some remote horizon, like parallels converging in infinity. The rhythm of history is conservative. Change is geologically slow. You must accept that. And accept as rightfully yours the happiness that comes your way.

LOUIS. But that's only half the picture, that's the ego-anarchist-cowboys-shrilling-for-no-government part of the Republicans but what about the other half, the religious fanatics who want to control every breath every citizen takes? I mean you say law isn't Justice and Justice isn't morals but really, who if not the Right is putting the Prude back in Jurisprudence?

JOE. No but see, there you go again! We're a movement, this is politics, not a representation of some pure force, it's . . . Do you want to be pure, or do you want to be effective? Choose. Even if our methods seem . . . extreme, even. We've worked hard to build a movement.

LOUIS. But McCarthyism. Watergate.

JOE kisses LOUIS.

LOUIS. Pat Buchanan. Jesse Helms.

JOE. Barry Goldwater.

They kiss.

JOE. George Will.

LOUIS. George Bush.

They kiss.

LOUIS. Newt Gingrich. Objectively speaking, a rum bunch.

JOE. Responsible for everything bad and evil in the World.

LOUIS. Throw Reagan on the pile and you're not far off.

JOE. Oh if people like you didn't have President Reagan to demonize where would you be?

LOUIS. If he didn't have people like me to demonize where would *he* be? Upper right-hand square on the Hollywood Squares.
This is interesting. I'm exploring my dark side these days, I'm losing myself in some ideological leather bar. The more appalling I find your politics the more I want to hump you. Bunker fucking; burn me up; may I never ever re-emerge.

Little pause.

JOE. I don't want to be punishment for you.

LOUIS. What do you want to be?

JOE. Um . . . A friend, I guess, a . . .

LOUIS. You are. Believe me. You protect me.
From all the buried and the unburied dead.
Let's spend the month in bed.

They start to fuck.

A week passes. HARPER *stands in a bra and panties and stockings.* HANNAH *in a bathrobe, has a dress over her arm. A pair of shoes stand ready nearby.*

HANNAH. Did you wash up?

HARPER *nods.*

HANNAH. Good.
  Now let's slip this on.

They put the dress on HARPER.

HANNAH. Good. It's pretty.
  Shoes?

HARPER *steps into them.*

Good. Now let's see about the hair.

HARPER *bends over,* HANNAH *combs* HARPER's *hair.*

At first it can be very hard to accept how disappointing life is, Harper, because that's what it is and you have to accept it. With faith and time and hard work you reach a point. . . . where the disappointment doesn't hurt as much, and then it gets actually easy to live with. Quite easy. Which is in its own way a disappointment. But.
  There.

HARPER (*angry*). I miss Joe's penis.

HANNAH. And I'm sure you'll understand it if I don't feel comfortable discussing that.

HARPER. It's five A.M., Mother Pitt. I hate this dress.

HANNAH. I get there first. I open up.
  I leave messages for him at his office. He leaves them for me.
  He won't come to the phone.
  I'll fix myself now. And we can go. (*She exits.*)

JOE. Freedom is where we bleed into one another. Right and Left. Freedom is the far horizon where lines converge. You will always have to make choices, and finally all life can offer you in the face of these terrible decisions is that you can make the choices freely. I did, I made a choice, I followed you. Louis. I came here. And this has taught me . . . To be less afraid. Because the courage to choose enabled me to find you.

LOUIS. And our fucking brought you to this Republican epiphany?

JOE. Do you think I'm stupid?

LOUIS. No.

JOE. A liar.

LOUIS. No.

JOE. What you did when you walked out on him was hard to do.
The world may not understand it or approve but it was *your*
choice, what *you* needed, not some fantasy Louis but *you*. You
did what you needed to do. And I consider you very brave.

LOUIS. Nobody does what I did, Joe. Nobody.

JOE. But maybe many want to. And maybe you should accept that
you wanted to, and let him go for real. Forget your victimology.
Forget that I am what I am and simply hear what I'm saying,
free from politics and history: You are in yourself a good, good
man. I admire you. I believe in you. I do.

LOUIS. I know you do.
    You seem to be able to live with what you've done, leaving
your wife, you're not all torn up and guilty, you've . . .
blossomed, but you're not a terrible person, you're a decent,
caring man. And I don't know how that's possible, but looking
at you it seems to be. You do seem free.

JOE. Yes.

LOUIS. And happy.

JOE. I am.

LOUIS. And at night you sleep peacefully. You don't have these
terrible, terrible, awful, horrible dreams

JOE. No. I never have any dreams at all.

Little pause. LOUIS *cries.*

Oh! Oh, you're . . . Louis, Louis I . . .

JOE *takes* LOUIS *in his arms, cradles him.*

LOUIS. I'm . . . stressed.
    No dreams at all. That would be amazing.
    I'm OK.

JOE. I'm sorry if I . . .

They kiss affectionately, romantically.

LOUIS. It's dawn, we should . . .

He lies down.

Make spoons.

JOE *complies.*

LOUIS. Sweet dreams. Or oblivion. Sweet, sweet oblivion.

A few seconds pass.

JOE (*very softly*). Louis?
    Louis?
    Louis?
    I love you.

HARPER *appears*.

HARPER. Don't worry, I'm not really here.
    I have terrible powers. I see more than I want to see. Maybe I'm a witch.

JOE. You're not.

HARPER. I could be a witch. Why not? I married a fairy.

JOE. Please, Harper, just go, I . . .

LOUIS (*waking from a drowse*). Joe . . . ?
    Are you OK?

JOE. Yeah, yeah, I . . . I have a screwy stomach. It's nothing.

HARPER (*simultaneously*). Talk softer, you're keeping him awake.
    Why am I here? You called me.

JOE. I didn't . . .

HARPER. You called me. Leave me alone if you're so goddamned happy.

JOE. I didn't call you.

HARPER. *THEN WHY AM I HERE?*

Pause. They look at each other.

HARPER. To see you again. Any way I can.
    You're a liar. You do so have dreams. Bad ones.
    OH GOD I WISH YOU WERE . . . No I don't. DEAD.
    Yes, I do .

LOUIS. Joe?

HARPER. You can't save him. You never saved anyone. Joe in love. Isn't it pathetic.

JOE. What?

HARPER. You're turning into me.

JOE. GO.

She vanishes.

LOUIS. What's . . .

JOE. Night chills. Nothing. I just can't sleep.

ACT TWO: The Epistle   February 1986

(For Sigrid Wurschmidt)

Scene One

PRIOR *and* BELIZE *after the funeral of a mutual friend, a major New York City drag-and-style queen. They stand outside a dilapidated funeral parlour on the Lower East Side.* BELIZE *is in defiantly bright and beautiful clothing.* PRIOR *is dressed oddly: a great long black coat and a huge, fringed, matching scarf, draped to a hood-like effect. His appearance is disconcerting, menacing, and vaguely redolent of the Biblical.*

In all the scenes that follow in which PRIOR *appears, this is his costume – he adds to and changes it slightly but it stays fundamentally corvine, ragged and eerie.*

Three weeks have passed since Act One.

PRIOR. It was tacky.

BELIZE. It was divine.
> He was one of the Great Glitter Queens. He couldn't be buried like a *civilian*. Trailing sequins and incense he came into the world, trailing sequins and incense he departed it. And good for him!

PRIOR. I thought the twenty professional Sicilian mourners were a bit much.

Little pause.

> A great queen; big fucking deal. That ludicrous spectacle in there, just a parody of the funeral of someone who *really* counted. We don't; faggots; we're just a bad dream the real world is having, and the real world's waking up. And he's *dead*.

Little pause.

BELIZE. Lately sugar you have gotten very strange. Lighten up already.

PRIOR. Oh I *apologise*, it was only a for-God's-sake funeral, a cause for fucking *celebration*, sorry if I can't join in with the rest of you death-junkies, gloating about your survival in the face of that . . . of his ugly demise because unlike you I have nothing to gloat about. Never mind.

Angry little pause.

BELIZE. And you *look* like Morticia Addams.

PRIOR. Like the Wrath of God.

BELIZE. Yes.

PRIOR. That is the intended effect.
    My eyes are fucked up.

BELIZE. Fucked up how?

PRIOR. Everything's . . . closing in. Weirdness on the periphery.

BELIZE. Since when?

PRIOR. For three weeks. Since that night. Since the night
    when . . . (*He stops himself.*)

BELIZE. Well what does the eye doctor say?

PRIOR. I haven't been.

BELIZE. Oh for *God's sake.* Why?

PRIOR. I was improving. Before.
    Remember my wet dream.

BELIZE. The angel?

PRIOR. It wasn't a dream.

BELIZE. 'Course it was.

PRIOR. No. I don't think so.
    I'm a prophet.

BELIZE. Say what?

PRIOR. I've been given a prophecy. A book. Not a *physical* book,
    or there was one but they took it back, but somehow there's still
    this book. In me. A prophecy. It . . . really happened, I'm . . .
    almost completely sure of it.

He looks at BELIZE.

Oh stop looking so . . .

BELIZE. You're scaring me.

PRIOR. It was after Louis left me. Every night I'd been having
    these horrible vivid dreams. And then . . .

Little pause.

BELIZE. Then . . . ?

PRIOR. And then She arrived.

Scene Two

The ANGEL *and* PRIOR *in* PRIOR's *bedroom, three weeks*
earlier: the wrecked ceiling, PRIOR *in the bed (he changes into*
his PJ's as he moves to it), the ANGEL *in the air.* BELIZE
watches from the street.

ANGEL. Greetings, Prophet!
    The Great Work Begins:
    The Messenger has arrived.

PRIOR. Go away.

ANGEL. Attend:

PRIOR. Oh God there's a thing in the air, a thing, a thing.

ANGEL. I I I I
    Am the Bird Of America, The Bald Eagle,
    Continental Principality,
    LUMEN PHOSPHOR FLUOR CANDLE!
    I unfold my leaves, Bright steel,
    In salutation open sharp before you:
    PRIOR WALTER
    Long-descended, well-prepared . . .

PRIOR. No, I'm not prepared, for anything, I have lots to do, I . . .

ANGEL (*with a gust of music*).
    American Prophet tonight you become,
    American Eye that pierceth Dark,
    American Heart all Hot for Truth,
    The True Great Vocalist, the Knowing Mind
    Tongue-of-the-Land, Seer-Head!

PRIOR. Oh, shoo! You're scaring the shit out me, get the fuck out
    of my room. Please, oh please . . .

ANGEL. Now:
    Remove from their hiding-place the Sacred Prophetic
    Implements.

    Little pause.

PRIOR. The *what*?

ANGEL. Remove from their hiding-place the Sacred Prophetic
    Implements.

    Little pause.

Your dreams have revealed them to you.

PRIOR. What dreams?

ANGEL. You have had dreams revealing to you . . .

PRIOR. I haven't had a dream I can remember in months.

ANGEL. No . . . dreams, you . . . Are you sure?

PRIOR. Yes. Well, the two dead Priors, they . . .

ANGEL. No not the heralds, not them. Other dreams. Implements, you must have . . . One moment.

PRIOR. *This*, this is a dream, obviously, I'm sick and so I . . . Well OK it's a pretty spectacular dream but still it's just some . . .

ANGEL. Quiet. Prophet. A moment, please, I . . . The disorganization is . . . (*She coughs, looks up.*) He says he hasn't had any . . . (*Coughs.*) Yes.
      In the kitchen. Under the tiles under the sink.

PRIOR. You want me to . . . to tear up the kitchen floor?

ANGEL. Get a shovel or an axe or some . . . tool for dislodging tile and grout and unearth the Sacred Implements.

PRIOR. No fucking way! The ceiling's bad enough, I'll lose the lease, I'll lose my security deposit, I'll wake up the downstairs neighbours, their hysterical dog, I . . . Do it yourself.

ANGEL (*a really terrifying voice*). SUBMIT, SUBMIT TO THE WILL OF HEAVEN!

An enormous gust of wind knocks PRIOR over. He glares at the ANGEL from the floor and shakes his head 'no.' A standoff. The ANGEL coughs a little. There is a small, soft explosion in the kitchen offstage. A cloud of plaster dust drifts on.

PRIOR. What did you . . . What . . . ? (*Exits into the kitchen.*)

ANGEL. And lo, the Prophet was led by his nightly dreams to the hiding-place of the Sacred Implements, and . . . Revision in the text: The Angel did help him to unearth them, for he was weak of body though not of will.

PRIOR returns with a very dusty ancient leather suitcase.

PRIOR. You cracked the refrigerator, you probably released a whole cloud of fluorocarbons, that's bad for the . . . the environment.

ANGEL. My wrath is as fearsome as my countenance is splendid. Open the suitcase.

PRIOR does. He reaches inside and produces a pair of bronze spectacles with rocks instead of lenses.

PRIOR. Oh, look at this. (*He puts them on.*)
  Like, wow, man, totally Paleozoic. This is . . .

He stops suddenly. His head jerks up. He is seeing something.

OH! OH GOD NO! OH . . . (*He tears off the spectacles.*)
  That was terrible! I don't want to see that!

ANGEL. Remove the Book.

PRIOR *removes a large book with bright steel pages from the suitcase. There is a really glorious burst of music, more light, more wind.*

ANGEL. From the Council of Continental Principalities
  Met in this time of Crisis and Confusion:
  Heaven here reaches down to disaster
  And in touching you touches all of Earth.

Music. She retrieves the spectacles, gives them to him.

ANGEL. Peep-stones.

He cautiously puts them on as:

ANGEL. Open me Prophet. I I I I am
  The Book.
  Read.

PRIOR. Wait. Wait. (*He takes off the glasses.*)
  How come . . . How come I have this . . . um, erection? It's very hard to concentrate.

ANGEL. The stiffening of your penis is of no consequence.

PRIOR. Well maybe not to you but . . .

ANGEL. READ! You are Mere Flesh. I I I I am Utter Flesh,
  Density of Desire, the Gravity of Skin:
  What makes the Engine of Creation Run?
  Not Physics But Ecstatics Makes The Engine Run:

The ANGEL's lines are continuous through this section. PRIOR's lines overlap. They both get very turned-on.

PRIOR (*hit by a wave of intense sexual feeling*). Hmmmm . . .

ANGEL. The Pulse, The Pull, The Throb, The Ooze . . .

PRIOR. Wait, please, I . . . Excuse me for just a minute, just a minute. OK I . . .

ANGEL. Priapsis, Dilation, Engorgement, Flow:
  The Universe Aflame with Angelic Ejaculate . . .

PRIOR (*losing control, he starts to hump the book*). Oh shit . . .

ANGEL. The Heavens A-thrum to the Seraphic Rut,

The Fiery Grapplings . . .

PRIOR. Oh God, I . . .

ANGEL. The Feathery Joinings of the Higher Orders,
     Infinite, Unceasing, The Blood-Pump Of Creation!

PRIOR. OH! OH! I . . . OH! Oh! Oh, oh . . .

ANGEL (*simultaneously*). HOLY Estrus! HOLY Orifice! Ecstasis
     in Excelsis! AMEN!

Pause. If they had cigarettes they'd smoke them now.

PRIOR. Oh. Oh God.

ANGEL. The Body is the Garden of the Soul.

PRIOR. What *was* that?

ANGEL. Plasma Orgasmata.

PRIOR. Yeah well no doubt.

BELIZE. Whoa whoa whoa wait a minute excuse me please. You
     fucked this angel?

PRIOR. She fucked me. She has . . . well, she has eight vaginas.

ANGEL. REGINA VAGINA!
     Hermaphroditically Equipped as well with a Bouquet of
     Phalli . . .
     I I I I am Your Released Female Essence Ascendant . . .

PRIOR (*to* BELIZE). The sexual politics of this are *very*
     confusing. God, for example is a man. Well, not a man, he's a
     flaming Hebrew letter.

ANGEL. The Aleph Glyph. Deus Erectus! Pater Omnipotens!

PRIOR. Angelic orgasm makes protomatter, which fuels the
     Engine of Creation. They used to copulate *ceaselessly*
     before . . .
     Each angel is an infinite aggregate myriad entity, they're
     basically incredibly powerful bureaucrats, they have no
     imagination, they can *do* anything but they can't invent,
     create, they're sort of fabulous and dull all at once.

ANGEL. Made for His Pleasure, We can only ADORE:
     Seeking something New . . .

PRIOR. God split the World in Two . . .

ANGEL. And made *YOU*.

PRIOR and ANGEL. Human Beings:
     Uni-Genitalled: Female. Male.

ANGEL. In creating You, Our Father-Lover unleashed

      Sleeping Creation's Potential For Change.
      In YOU the Virus of TIME began!

PRIOR. In making us God apparently set in motion a potential in the design for change, for random event, for movement forward.

ANGEL. YOU *Think*. And You *IMAGINE!*
      Migrate, Explore, and when you do:

PRIOR. As the human race began to progress, travel, intermingle, everything started to come unglued. Manifest first as tremors in Heaven.

ANGEL. Heaven is a City Much Like San Francisco.
      House upon House depended from hillside,
      From Crest down to Dockside,
      The green Mirroring Bay:

PRIOR. And there are earthquakes there, or rather, heavenquakes.

ANGEL. Oh Joyful in the Buckled Garden,
      Undulant Landscape Over Which
      The Threat Of Seismic Catastrophe hangs,
      More beautiful because imperilled.
      POTENT: yet DORMANT: The Fault Lines of Creation!

BELIZE. So Human progress . . .

PRIOR. Migration. Science. Forward Motion.

BELIZE. . . . . shakes up Heaven.

ANGEL. Paradise itself Shivers and Splits,
      Each day when You awake, as though WE are only the
          Dream of YOU.
      PROGRESS! MOVEMENT!
      Shaking *HIM*:

BELIZE. God.

ANGEL. He began to leave us!
      Bored with His Angels, Bewitched by Humanity,
      In Mortifying Imitation of You, his least creation,
      He would sail off on Voyages, no knowing where.
      Quake follows quake,
      Absence follows Absence:
      Nasty Chastity and Disorganization:
      Loss of Libido, Protomatter Shortfall:
      We are his Functionaries; it is
      BEYOND US:
      Then:
      April 18, 1906.
      In That Day:

PRIOR. The Great San Francisco Earthquake. And also . . .

ANGEL. *In that day:*

PRIOR (*simultaneously*). On April 18, 1906 . . .

ANGEL. Our Lover of the Million Unutterable Names,
      The Aleph Glyph from Which all Words Descend:
      The King of the Universe:
      HE Left

PRIOR. Abandoned.

ANGEL. *And did not return.*
      We do not know where HE has gone. HE may *never* . . .
      And bitter, cast-off, We wait, bewildered;
      Our finest houses, our sweetest vineyards,
      Made drear and barren, missing Him.

   Coughs.

BELIZE. Abandoned.

PRIOR. Yes.

BELIZE. I smell a motif. The man that got away.

PRIOR. Well it occurred to me. Louis.
      Even now, if he came back I'd . . . (*He shrugs.*)

BELIZE. Listen to your girlfriend.
      I think the time has come to let him go.

PRIOR. That's not what the angels think, they think . . . It's all
   gone too far, too much loss is what they think, we should stop
   somehow, go back.

BELIZE. But that's not how the world works, Prior. It only spins
   forward.

PRIOR. Yeah but forward into *what*?

ANGEL. Surely you see towards what We are Progressing:
      The fabric of the sky unravels:
      Angels hover, anxious fingers worry
      The tattered edge.
      Before the boiling of blood and the searing of skin
      Comes the Secret Catastrophe:
      Before Life on Earth becomes finally merely impossible,
      It will for a long time before have become completely
         unbearable.

   Coughs.

   YOU HAVE DRIVEN HIM AWAY! YOU MUST STOP
   MOVING!

PRIOR (*quiet, terrified*). Stop moving.

ANGEL (*softly*). Forsake the Open Road:
  Neither Mix Nor Intermarry: Let Deep Roots Grow:
  If you do not MINGLE you will Cease to Progress:
  Seek Not to Fathom the World and its Delicate Particle Logic:
  You cannot Understand, You can only Destroy,
  You do not Advance, You only Trample.
  Poor blind Children, abandoned on the Earth,
  Groping terrified, misguided, over
  Fields of Slaughter, over bodies of the Slain:
  HOBBLE YOURSELVES!
  There is No Zion Save Where You Are!
  If you Cannot find your Heart's desire . . .

PRIOR. In your own back yard . . .

ANGEL, PRIOR and BELIZE. You never lost it to begin with.

The ANGEL *coughs.*

ANGEL. Turn back. Undo.
  Till HE returns again.

PRIOR. Please. Please. Angel or dream, whatever you are . . .

BELIZE. It's a dream, baby . . .

PRIOR. Whatever you are, I don't understand this visitation, I
  don't understand what you want from me, I'm not a prophet,
  I'm a sick lonely man, I . . .
    What are you? Did you come here to save me or destroy
  me? Stop. Moving. That's what you want. Answer me! You
  want me dead.

Pause. The ANGEL *and* PRIOR *look at each other.*

ANGEL. YES. NO. NO.

Coughs.

This is not in the Text, We *deviate* . . .
  No more.

She picks up the Book.

PRIOR. *I. WANT.* You to go away. I'm tired to death of being
  done to, walked out on, *infected*, fucked over and *now* tortured
  by some mixed-up, irresponsible angel, some . . . Leave me
  alone.

The ANGEL *lands in front of* PRIOR.

ANGEL. You can't Outrun your Occupation, Jonah.
  Hiding from Me one place you will find me in another.
  I I I I stop down the road, waiting for you.

She touches him, tenderly, and turns him, cradling him with one arm.

ANGEL. You Know Me Prophet: Your battered heart,
    Bleeding Life in the Universe of Wounds.

The ANGEL presses the volume against his chest. They both experience something unnameable – painful, joyful in equal measure. There is a terrifying sound. The ANGEL gently, lovingly lowers PRIOR to the ground.

ANGEL. Vessel of the BOOK now: Oh Exemplum Paralyticum:
    On you in you in your blood we write have written:
        STASIS!
    The END.

In gales of music, holding the Book aloft, the ANGEL ascends. The bedroom disappears. PRIOR stands, puts on his street clothes, and resumes his place beside BELIZE. They are back on the street in front of the funeral home.

BELIZE. You have been spending too much time alone.

PRIOR. Not by choice. None of this by choice.

BELIZE. This is . . . worse than nuts, it's . . . well, don't migrate, don't mingle, that's . . . malevolent, some of us didn't exactly *choose* to migrate, know what I'm saying . . .

PRIOR (*overlapping*). I hardly think it's appropriate for you to get *offended*, I didn't invent this shit, it was *visited* on me . . .

BELIZE (*overlapping on 'offended'*). But it *is* offensive or at least monumentally confused and it's not . . . visited, Prior. By who? It *is* from you, what else is it?

PRIOR. Something else.

BELIZE. That's crazy.

PRIOR. Then I'm crazy.

BELIZE. No, you're . . .

PRIOR. Then it was an angel.

BELIZE. It was *not* an . . .

PRIOR. Then I'm crazy. The whole world is, why not me? It's 1986 and there's a *plague*, half my friends are dead and I'm only thirty-one, every goddamn morning I wake up and I think Louis is next to me in the bed and it takes me long minutes to remember . . . that this is *real*, it isn't just an impossible, terrible dream, so maybe yes I'm flipping out.

BELIZE (*angry*). You better not. You better fucking not flip out. This is not dementia. And this is not real. This is just you,

Prior, afraid of the future, afraid of time. Longing to go
backwards so bad you made this angel up, a cosmic reactionary.
But there's no angel. You hear me?
For me? I can handle anything but not this happening to you.

PRIOR. Maybe I am a prophet. Not just me, all of us who are
dying now. Maybe we've caught the virus of prophecy. Be still.
Toil no more. Maybe the world has driven God from Heaven,
incurred the angels' wrath.

ANGEL'S VOICE. Whisper into the ear of the World, Prophet,
Wash up red in the tide of its dreams,
And billow bloody words into the sky of sleep.

PRIOR. I believe I've seen the end of things. And having seen, I'm
going blind, as prophets do. It makes a certain sense to me.

ANGEL'S VOICE. FOR THIS AGE OF ANOMY: A NEW
LAW!

PRIOR. And if I hate heaven my only resistance is to run.

ANGEL'S VOICE. Delivered this night, this silent night, from
Heaven,
Oh Prophet, to You.

ACT THREE: Borborygmi

(The Squirming Facts Exceed the Squamous Mind)

February 1986

Scene One

A week later. ROY *in his hospital room. The pain in his gut is now constant and getting worse. He is on the phone, a more elaborate phone than in the previous scene. Legal documents and files are strewn on the bed.*

At the foot of the bed is a small, locked icebox.

ROY. No records no records what are you deaf I said I have no records for their shitty little committee, it's not how I work I . . .

He has an incredibly bad abdominal spasm; he's in great pain. He holds the phone away, grimaces terribly, curls up into a ball and then uncurls, all the while making no sound.

ETHEL *appears in her hat and coat, walks to a chair by the bed and sits, watching* ROY, *silent. He watches her enter, and then resumes his phone call, never taking his eyes off her.*

ROY. Those notes were lost. LOST. In a fire, water damage, I can't do this any . . .

BELIZE *enters with a pill-tray.*

(*To* BELIZE). I threw up fifteen times today! I *COUNTED*.
(*Pause. To* ETHEL.) What are *you* looking at?
(*To* BELIZE.) Fifteen times.

(*He goes back to the phone.*) Yeah?

BELIZE. Hang up the phone, I have to watch you take these . . .

ROY. The LIMO thing? Oh for the love of Christ I was acquitted twice for that, they're trying to kill me dead with this *harassment*, I have done things in my life but I never killed anyone.
(*To* ETHEL.) Present company excepted. And you *deserved* it.
(*To* BELIZE.) Get the fuck outa here.
(*Back to the phone.*) Stall. It can't start tomorrow if we don't show, so don't show, I'll pay the old harridan back. I have to have a . . .

BELIZE. Put down the phone.

ROY. Suck my dick, Mother Teresa, this is life and death.

BELIZE. Put down the . . .

> ROY *snatches the pill cup off the tray and throws the pills on the floor.* BELIZE *reaches for the phone.* ROY *slams down the receiver and snatches the phone away.*

ROY. You touch that phone and I'll bite. And I got rabies.
    And from now on, I supply my own pills. I already told 'em to push their jujubes to the losers down the hall.

BELIZE. Your own pills.

ROY. No double-blind. A little bird warned me. The vultures . . . (*Another severe spasm. This time he makes noise.*) Jesus God these cramps, now I know why women go berserk once a . . . AH FUCK!

He has another spasm. ETHEL *laughs.*

ROY. Oh good I made her laugh.

The pain is slightly less. He's a little calmer.

I don't trust this hospital. For all I know Lillian fucking *Hellman* is down in the basement switching the pills around – no, wait, she's dead, isn't she. Oh boy, memory, it's – . Hey Ethel, didn't Lillian die, did you see her up there, ugly, ugly broad, nose like a . . . like even a Jew should worry mit a punim like that. You seen somebody fitting that description up there in Red Heaven? Hah?
    She won't talk to me. She thinks she's some sort of a deathwatch or something.

BELIZE. Who are you talking to?

ROY. I'm self-medicating.

BELIZE. With what?

ROY (*trying to remember*). Acid something.

BELIZE. Azidothymedine?

ROY. Gezundheit.

> ROY *tosses a ring of keys to* BELIZE.

BELIZE. AZT? You got . . . ?

He unlocks the ice-box; it's full of bottles of pills.

ROY. One hundred proof elixir vitae.
    Give me the keys.

BELIZE. You scored.

ROY. Impressively.

BELIZE. Lifetime supply.

There are maybe thirty people in the whole country who are getting this drug.

ROY. Now there are thirty-one.

BELIZE. There are a hundred thousand people who need it.

Look at you. The dragon atop the golden horde. It's not fair, is it?

ROY. No, but as Jimmy Carter said, neither is life. So put your brown eyes back in your goddam head, baby, I am not moved by an unequal distribution of goods on this earth. It's history, I didn't write it though I flatter myself I am a footnote. And you are a nurse, so minister and skedaddle.

BELIZE. If you live fifty more years you won't swallow all these pills.

Pause.

I want some.

ROY. That's illegal.

BELIZE. Ten bottles.

ROY. I'm gonna report you.

BELIZE. There's a nursing shortage. I'm in a union. I'm real scared. I have friends who need them. Bad.

ROY. Loyalty I admire. But no.

BELIZE (*amazed, off-guard*). Why?

Pause.

ROY. Because you repulse me. '*WHY*?' You'll be begging for it next. '*WHY*?' Because I hate your guts, and your friends' guts, that's *why*. 'Gimme!' So goddamned entitled. Such a shock when the bill comes due.

BELIZE. From what I read you never paid a fucking bill in your life.

ROY. *No one* has worked harder than me. To end up knocked flat in a . . .

BELIZE (*overlapping*). Yeah well things are tough all over.

ROY (*continues over* BELIZE). And you come *here* looking for *fairness*? (*To* ETHEL.) They couldn't touch me when I was alive, and now when I am dying they try this: (*He grabs up all the paperwork in two fists.*) Now! When I'm a . . . (*Back to* BELIZE.) That's fair? What am I? A dead man!

A terrible spasm, quick and violent; he doubles up.

Fuck! What was I saying Oh God I can't remember any . . . Oh yeah, dead.

   I'm a goddam dead man.

BELIZE. You expect *pity*?

ROY (*a beat, then*). I expect you to hand over those keys and move your nigger ass out of my room.

BELIZE. What did you say.

ROY. Move your nigger cunt spade faggot lackey ass out of my room.

BELIZE (*overlapping starting on 'spade'*). Shit-for-brains filthy-mouthed selfish motherfucking cowardly cocksucking cloven-hoofed pig.

ROY (*overlapping*). Mongrel. Dinge. Slave. Ape.

BELIZE. Kike.

ROY. *Now* you're talking!

BELIZE. Greedy Kike.

ROY. Now you can have a bottle. But only one.

   BELIZE *tosses the keys at* ROY, *hard*. ROY *catches them.* BELIZE *takes a bottle of the pills, then another, then a third, and leaves. As soon as he is out of the room* ROY *is wracked with a series of spasms; he's been holding them in.*

ROY. GOD I thought he'd never go!

   (*To* ETHEL). So what? Are you going to sit there all night?

ETHEL. Till morning.

ROY. Uh huh. The cock crows, you go back to the swamp.

ETHEL. No. I take the 7.05 to Yonkers.

ROY. What the fuck's in Yonkers?

ETHEL. The disbarment committee hearings. You been hocking about it all week. I'll have a look-see.

ROY. They won't let you in the front door. You're a convicted and executed traitor.

ETHEL. I'll walk through a wall.

   She starts to laugh. He joins her.

ROY. Fucking SUCCUBUS! Fucking blood-sucking old bat!

   He picks up the phone, punches a couple of buttons and then puts the receiver back, dejectedly.

The worst thing about being sick in America, Ethel, is you are·
booted out of the parade. Americans have no use for sick. Look
at Reagan: He's so healthy he's hardly human, he's a hundred if
he's a day, he takes a slug in his chest and two days later he's
out west riding ponies in his PJ's. I mean who does that? That's
America. It's just no country for the infirm.

Scene Two

*Later the same day. The Diorama Room of the Mormon Visitors'
Centre. The diorama is in a little proscenium theatre; the curtains
are drawn shut. There are nice seats for the audience; and
HARPER is in one of them, dressed the same as in her last scene.
She has bags of potato chips and M&M's and cans of soda
scattered all around. HANNAH enters with PRIOR.*

HANNAH. This is the Diorama Room.

(*To* HARPER.) I thought we agreed that you weren't . . .

(*To* PRIOR.) I'll go see if I can get it started.

*She exits. PRIOR sits. The lights in the room dim. A Voice on
tape intones.*

VOICE. Welcome to the Mormon Visitors' Centre Diorama
Room. In a moment, our show will begin. We hope it will have
a special message for you. Please refrain from smoking, and
food and drink are not allowed. (*A chiming tone.*) Welcome to
the Mormon Visitors' . . .

*The tape lurches into very high speed, then smears into
incomprehensibly low speed, then stops, mid-message, with an
unpromising metallic blat.*

HARPER. They're having trouble with the machinery.

*She rips open a bag of nacho-flavoured Doritos and offers
them to PRIOR.*

PRIOR. You're not supposed to eat in the . . .

HARPER. I can. I live here. Have we met before?

PRIOR. No, I don't . . . think so. You *live* here?

HARPER. There's a dummy family in the diorama, you'll see
when the curtain opens. The main dummy, the big daddy
dummy, looks like my husband, Joe. When they push the

buttons he'll start to talk. You can't believe a word he says but the sound of him is reassuring. It's an *incredible* resemblance.

PRIOR. Are you a Mormon?

HARPER. Jack Mormon.

PRIOR. I beg your pardon?

HARPER. Jack Mormon. It means I'm flawed. Inferior Mormon product. Probably comes from jack rabbit, you know, I *ran*.

PRIOR. Do you believe in angels? In the Angel Mormon?

HARPER. Moroni, not Mormon, The Angel Moroni. Ask my mother in-law, when you leave, the scary lady at the reception desk, if its name was Moroni why don't they call themselves Morons. It's from comments like that you can tell I'm jack Mormon. You're not a Mormon.

PRIOR. No, I . . .

HARPER. Just . . . distracted with grief.

PRIOR. I'm not. I was just walking and . . .

HARPER. We get a lot of distracted, grief-stricken people here. It's our specialty.

PRIOR. I'm not . . . distracted, I'm doing research.

HARPER. On Mormons?

PRIOR. On . . . Angels. I'm a . . . An Angelologist.

HARPER. I never met an angelologist before.

PRIOR. It's an obscure discipline.

HARPER. I can imagine. Angelology. The fieldwork must be rigorous. You'd have to drop dead before you saw your first specimen.

PRIOR. One . . . I saw one. An angel. It crashed through my bedroom ceiling.

HARPER. Huh. That sort of thing always happens to me.

PRIOR. I have a fever. I should be in bed but I'm too anxious to lie in bed. You look *very* familiar.

HARPER. So do you.
    But it's just not possible. I don't get out. I've only ever been here, or in some place a lot like this, alone, in the dark, waiting for the dummy.

The lights in the Diorama Room darken; dramatic music; the curtains part and lights up on the little stage, where a classic wagon-train tableau posed before a painted backdrop: a covered wagon and a Mormon family in the desert on the great trek from Missouri to Salt Lake. The family members are historically-dressed mannequins: two sons, a mother and a daughter, and the father (who is actually the actor playing JOE). *The Voice on tape again.*

VOICE. In 1847, across fifteen hundred miles of frontier wilderness, braving mountain blizzards, desert storms, and renegade Indians, The first Mormon wagon trains made their difficult way towards the Kingdom of God.

HARPER. Want some nacho-flavoured . . . Hi Joe.

The diorama comes to life. Sounds of a wagon train, the Largo from Dvorak's Ninth Symphony. The boy dummies, CALEB and ORRIN, don't talk, you just hear their voices on a tape, and a pin-spot hits their faces to indicate who is talking: the effect is unintentionally eerie. The FATHER's face moves but not his body.

CALEB (*voice on tape*). Father, I'm a-feard.

FATHER. Hush, Caleb.

ORRIN (*voice on tape*). The wilderness is so vast.

FATHER Orrin, Caleb, hush. Be brave for your mother and your little sister.

CALEB. We'll try, Father, we want you to be proud of us. We want to be brave and strong like you.

HARPER (*simultaneously*). They don't have any lines, the sister and the mother. And only his face moves. That's not really fair.

ORRIN. When will we arrive in Zion, father? When will our great exodus finally be done? All this wandering . . .

HARPER (*overlapping on 'Father'*). Never. You'll die of snake bite and your brother looks like scorpion food to me.

FATHER (*overlapping on 'scorpion'*). Soon boys, soon, just like the Prophet promised. The Lord leads the way.

CALEB. Will there be lots to eat there, Father?

HARPER (*on 'Father'*). No, just sand.

CALEB (*continuous*). Will the desert flow with milk and honey? Will there be water there?

HARPER (*on 'water'*). Oh, there's a big lake but it's *salt*, that's the joke. . .

FATHER (*on 'joke'*). The Lord will provide for us, son, he always has.

ORRIN. Well, not *always* . . .

HARPER (*continuous over above*) . . . they drag you on your knees through hell and when you get there the water of course is undrinkable. Salt. It's a Promised Land, but *what* a disappointing promise!

FATHER (*on 'promise'*). Sometimes He tests us, son, that's His way, but . . .

CALEB. Read to us, father, read us the story!

FATHER (*chuckles*). Again?

SONS. Yes! Yes! The Story! The Story! The story about the Prophet!

HARPER (*simultaneously*). The story! The story! The story about the Prophet!

FATHER. Well boys, well:
    1823, the Prophet, who was a strapping lad, like everyone else in his time was seeking God, there were many churches, disputatious enough but who was Right? Could only be One True Church. All else darkness . . .

    LOUIS *suddenly appears in the Diorama.*

LOUIS. But how can a fundamentally theocratic religion exist in a pluralist democracy, I mean . . .

JOE. I'm busy, Louis.

LOUIS. But . . . A *Mormon*? You're a . . . a . . . a . . .

JOE. Mormon. Yes.

LOUIS. But you . . . you *can't* be a Mormon! You're a lawyer! A *serious* lawyer!

PRIOR. Oh my god Oh my god. What . . .What is going on here?

JOE (*simultaneously*). The chief clerk of the Chief Justice of the Supreme Court is . . .

HARPER. You know him?

PRIOR (*closing his eyes*). I'm delirious, I must be delirious.

LOUIS(*looking around*). God you should get a bigger office, it's crowded in . . . I don't like cults.

JOE. The Church of Jesus Christ of Latter Day Saints is not a cult.

LOUIS. Any religion that's not at least two thousand years old is a cult.

PRIOR. WHAT IS HE DOING IN THERE?

JOE (*simultaneously*). Oh shut up, Louis.

LOUIS. And I know people who would call *that* generous.

PRIOR. WHAT IS HE . . .

HARPER. Who? The little creep? He's in and out every day. I hate him. He's got absolutely *nothing* to do with the story.

PRIOR. Can you turn it off? The . . . I'm leaving, I can't . . .

LOUIS. Why didn't you tell me that you . . .

JOE. It's a surprise?

LOUIS. No, no most of the men I go to bed with turn out to be YEAH OF COURSE it's a surprise! I thought you were all out west somewhere with the salt flats and the cactuses. There's some sort of profound displacement going on here, I . . .

PRIOR. Louis.

LOUIS (*hearing him*). Did you . . .

JOE. What?

LOUIS. I thought I heard . . . Somebody. Prior.

(*To* JOE.) We have to talk.

JOE. I'm working.

LOUIS. Fuck it. This is a crisis. Now.

LOUIS *exits.* JOE *sighs and then follows.*

HARPER. Well the dummy never *left* with the little creep, he never left before. When they come in and they see he's gone, they'll blame me.

HARPER *goes to the diorama stage and pulls its bright red curtain closed. She turns back and sees that* PRIOR *is crying.*

You shouldn't do that in here, this isn't a place for real feelings, this is just storytime here, stop.

PRIOR. I never imagined losing my mind was going to be such hard work.

HARPER. Oh, it is.

Find someplace else to be miserable in. This is *my* place and I don't want you to do that here!

PRIOR. I JUST SAW MY LOVER, MY . . . ex-lover, with a . . . with your husband, with that . . . window-display Ken doll, in that . . . *thing*, I saw him, I . . .

HARPER. Well don't have a hissy fit, I told you it wasn't working right, it's just . . . the magic of the theatre or something. Listen, if you see the creep, tell him to bring Joe . . . to bring the mannequin back, they'll evict me and this is it, it's nothing but it's the last place on earth for me. I can't go sit in Brooklyn.

HANNAH *enters.*

HANNAH. What's all the . . .

She sees PRIOR *crying. She glares at* HARPER.

What did you do to him?

HARPER. Nothing! He just can't *adjust*, is all, he just . . .

HANNAH *has gone to the diorama. She yanks the curtain open.*

HARPER. NO WAIT, Don't . . .

The FATHER *dummy is back – a real dummy this time.*

HARPER. Oh. (*To* PRIOR.) Look, we . . . imagined it.

HANNAH. This is a favour, they let me work here as a favour, but you keep making scenes, and look at this mess, it's a garbage scow!

HARPER (*over* HANNAH, *to* PRIOR). It doesn't look so much like him, now. He's changed. Again.

HANNAH (*overlapping*). Are you just going to sit here forever, trash piling higher, day after day till . . . Well till what?

HARPER (*overlapping*). You sound just like him. You even grind your teeth in your sleep like him.

HANNAH (*overlapping*). If I could get him to come back I would go back to Salt Lake tomorrow but I know my duty when I see it, and if you and Joe could say the same we . . .

HARPER (*overlapping on 'Salt Lake'*). You can't go back to Salt Lake, you sold your house! (*To* PRIOR.) My mother-in-law! She sold her house! Her son calls and tells her he's a homo and what does she do? She sells her house! And she calls *me* crazy! (*To* HANNAH.) You have less of a place in this world than I do if that's possible.

PRIOR. Am I dreaming this, I don't understand.

HARPER. He saw an angel.

HANNAH. That's his business.

HARPER. He's an angelologist.

PRIOR. Well don't go blabbing about it.

HANNAH. If you aren't serious you shouldn't come in here.

HARPER (*simultaneously*). Either that or he's nuts.

PRIOR. It's a visitors' centre; I'm visiting.

HARPER. He has a point.

HANNAH (*to* HARPER). Quiet!

(*To* PRIOR.) It's for serious visitors, it's a serious religion.

PRIOR. Do they like, *pay* you to do this?

HARPER. She volunteers.

PRIOR. Because you're not very hospitable. I did see an angel.

HANNAH. And what do you want me to do about it? I have problems of my own.
The diorama's closed for repairs. You have to leave.

(*To* HARPER.) Clean up this mess. (*Exits.*)

Embarrassed little pauses, then:

HARPER (*pointing to the* MORMON MOTHER). His wife. His mute wife. I'm waiting for her to speak. Bet her story's not so jolly.

PRIOR. Imagination is a dangerous thing.

HARPER. (*looking at the* FATHER *dummy*). In certain circumstances, fatal. It can blow up in your face. If it turns out to be true. Threshold . . . .

PRIOR and HARPER. . . . . of revelation.

They look at each other.

PRIOR. It's crazy time. I feel . . . this is nuts. I feel . . . this is nuts. We've never met, but I feel you know me incredibly well.

HARPER. Crazy time. The barn door's open now, and all the cows have fled. You don't look well. You really should be home in bed.

PRIOR. I'll die there.

HARPER. Better in bed than on the street. Just ask anyone.
Till we meet again.

PRIOR *leaves.* HARPER *sits alone.*

Bitter lady of the Plains, talk to me. Tell me what to do.

The MORMON MOTHER *turns to* HARPER, *then stands and leaves the diorama stage. She gestures with her head for* HARPER *to follow her.*

HARPER. I'm stuck. My heart's an anchor.

MORMON MOTHER. Leave it, then. Can't carry no extra weight.

The MORMON MOTHER *steps out of the diorama, crosses to where* HARPER *is sitting.* HARPER *sits a moment. She goes to the diorama, gets in the* MORMON MOTHER*'s seat.*

HARPER (*to the dummy* FATHER). Look at us. So perfect in place. The desert the mountains the previous century. Maybe I could have believed in you then. Maybe we should never have moved east.

MORMON MOTHER. Come on.

They exit.

Scene Three

Late that afternoon. JOE *and* LOUIS *sitting shoulder to shoulder in the dunes at Jones Beach, facing the ocean. It's cold. The sound of waves and gulls and distant Belt Parkway traffic. New York Romantic.* JOE *is very cold,* LOUIS *as always is oblivious to the weather.*

JOE. Louis . . . ?

LOUIS. The winter Atlantic. Wow, huh? .

JOE. Ferocious. It's freezing, what are we . . .

LOUIS. There used to be guys in the dunes even when it snowed. Nothing deterred us from the task at hand.

JOE. Which was?

LOUIS. Exploration. Across an unmapped terrain. The body of the homosexual human male. Here, or the Ramble, or the scrub pines on Fire Island, or the St. Mark's Baths. Hardy pioneers. Like your ancestors.

JOE. Not exactly.

LOUIS And many have perished on the trail.
    I fucked around a whole lot more than he did. So why is he the sick one? No justice. Anyway I wanted you to see this.

JOE. Why?

LOUIS. No reason.

Little pause.

JOE. I love you.

LOUIS. No you don't.

JOE. Yes I do.

LOUIS. NO YOU DON'T. You think you do but that's just the gay virgin thing, that's . . .

JOE (*tousling* LOUIS'*s hair*). Stop working so hard.
Listen to the ocean.
I love it when you can get to places and see what it used to be. The whole country was like this once. A paradise.

LOUIS. Ruined now.

JOE. It's a great country. Best place on earth. Best place to be.

LOUIS. I can't believe you're a Mormon. You never told me.

JOE. You never asked.

LOUIS. You said you were a Protestant.

JOE. I am. Sort of.

LOUIS. So what else haven't you told me?
So the fruity underwear you wear, that's . . . .

JOE. A temple garment.

LOUIS. Oh my god. What's it for?

JOE. Protection. A second skin. I can stop wearing it if you . . .

LOUIS. How can you stop wearing it if it's a skin? Your past, your beliefs, your . . .

JOE. I'm not your enemy. Louis.
I do . . . I am in love with you.
You and I, fundamentally, we're the same. We both want the same things.

LOUIS. I want to see Prior again.

JOE *stands up, moves away.*

LOUIS. I miss him, I . . .

JOE. You want to go back to . . .

LOUIS. I just . . . Need to see him again.

Little pause.

Don't you . . . You must want to see your wife.

JOE. I do see her. All the time. (*Pointing to his head.*) In here.
I miss her, I feel bad for her, I . . . I'm afraid of her.

LOUIS. Yes.

JOE. And I want more to be with . . .

LOUIS. I have to. See him. It's like a bubble rising up through rock, it's taken time, I don't know, the month in bed and the . . .

Love is still what I don't get, it . . . never seems to fit into any of the schematics, wherever I'm going and whatever I've prepared for I always seem to have forgotten about love.

I only know. . . . It's an unsafe thing. To talk about love, Joe. Please don't look so sad.

I just. I have to see him again. Do you understand what I . . .

JOE. You don't want to see me anymore.

Louis.

Anything. Whatever you want. I can give up anything. My skin.

He starts to remove his clothes. LOUIS, *when he realizes what* JOE *is doing, tries to stop him.*

LOUIS. What are you doing, someone will see us, it's not a nude beach, it's freezing!

JOE *is half-in, half-out of his clothes. He has pulled the upper part of the garment off.*

JOE. I'm flayed.

No past now. I could give up anything . Maybe . . . in what we've been doing, maybe I'm even infected.

LOUIS. No you're . . .

JOE. I don't want to be. I want to live now. And I can be anything I need to be. And I want to be with you.

LOUIS *starts to dress* JOE.

JOE (*as he's being dressed*). You have a good heart and you think the good thing is to be guilty and kind always but it's not always kind to be gentle and soft, there's a genuine violence softness and weakness visit on people. Sometimes self-interested is the most generous thing you can be.

You ought to think about that.

LOUIS. I will. Think about it.

JOE. You ought to think about . . . what you're doing to me. No, I mean . . . What you need. Think about what *you* need . Be brave.

And then you'll come back to me.

Scene Four

Night of the same day. LOUIS *and* JOE *remain onstage from the previous scene.*

ROY*'s hospital room.* ROY *is asleep.* BELIZE *enters, carrying a tray and a glass of water. He wakes* ROY *up.*

BELIZE. Time to take your pills.

ROY (*waking*). What? What time of . . .
      Water.

   BELIZE *gives him a glass of water.*

ROY. Bitter.
      Look out there. Black midnight.

BELIZE. You want anything?

ROY. Nothing that comes from there. As far as I'm concerned you
   can take all that away.

   Seeing BELIZE.

   Oh . . .

BELIZE. What?

ROY. Oh. The bogeyman is here.
      Lookit, a schvartze toytenmann.
      Come in, sweetheart, what took you so long?

BELIZE. You're flying, Roy. It's the morphine. They put
   morphine in the drip to stop the . . . You awake? Can you see
   who I am?

ROY. Oh yeah, you came for my mama, years ago.
      You wrap your arms around me now. Squeeze the bloody
   life from me. OK?

BELIZE. Uh, no, it's not OK. You're stoned, Roy.

ROY. Dark strong arms, take me like that. Deep and sincere but
   not too rough, just open me up to the end of me.

BELIZE. Who am I, Roy?

ROY. The Negro night nurse, my negation. You've come to escort
   me to the underworld. (*A serious sexual invitation.*) Come on.

BELIZE. You want me in your bed, Roy? You want me to take
   you away.

ROY. I'm ready . . .

BELIZE. I'll be coming for you soon. Everything I want is in the end of you.

ROY. So *now. God*, I'm ready.
  Fucking slow like every black man.
  Let me ask you something, sir.

BELIZE. *Sir?*

ROY. What's it like? After?

BELIZE. After . . . ?

ROY. This misery ends.

BELIZE. Hell or Heaven?

  ROY *stares at* BELIZE.

BELIZE. Like San Francisco.

ROY. A city. Good. I was worried . . . it'd be a garden. I hate that shit.

BELIZE. Mmmm.
  Big city, overgrown with weeds, but flowering weeds. On every corner a wrecking crew and something new and crooked going up catty-corner to that. Windows missing in every edifice like broken teeth, fierce gusts of gritty wind, and a grey high sky full of ravens.

ROY. Isaiah.

BELIZE. Prophet birds, Roy.
  Piles of trash, but lapidary like rubies and obsidian, and diamond-coloured cowspit streamers in the wind. And voting booths.

ROY. And a dragon atop a golden horde.

BELIZE. And everyone in Balenciaga gowns with red corsages, and big dance palaces full of music and lights and racial impurity and gender confusion.

  ROY *laughs softly, delighted.*

BELIZE. And all the deities are creole, mulatto, brown as the mouths of rivers.

  Roy *laughs again.*

BELIZE. Race, taste and history finally overcome.
  And you ain't there.

ROY (*happily shaking his head 'no' in agreement*). And Heaven?

BELIZE. That *was* Heaven, Roy.

ROY. The fuck it was.
   (*Suspicious, frightened.*) *Who are you?*

   Little pause.

BELIZE (*whispering*). I work for the KGB.

ROY. You and Paul Robeson. (*Trying to get his head clear.*) Do I know you.

BELIZE. Your negation.

ROY. Yeah. I know you. Nothing. A stomach grumble that wakes you in the night. A dark place created in the absence of me.

   ETHEL *enters.*

BELIZE. Been nice talking to you. Go to sleep now, baby. I'm just the shadow on your grave.

Scene Five

HARPER *and the* MORMON MOTHER. *Night. At the Brooklyn Heights Promenade. Everyone from the previous two scenes remains onstage.*

HARPER. It's not safe to be out on the street here, there are crazy people around.

MORMON MOTHER (*looking at the skyline*). Towers filled with fire. It's the Great Beyond.

HARPER. Manhattan. Was it a hard thing, crossing the prairies?

MORMON MOTHER. You ain't stupid. So don't ask stupid. Ask something for real.

HARPER (*a beat, then*). In your experience of the world. How do people change?

MORMON MOTHER. Well it has something to do with God so it's not very nice.
   God splits the skin with a jagged thumbnail from throat to belly and then plunges a huge filthy hand in, he grabs hold of your bloody tubes and they slip to evade his grasp but he squeezes hard, he *insists*, he pulls and pulls till all your innards are yanked out and the pain! We can't even talk about that. And then he stuffs them back, dirty, tangled and torn. It's up to you to do the stitching.

HARPER. And then get up. And walk around.

MORMON MOTHER. Just mangled guts pretending.

HARPER. That's how people change.

> PRIOR *appears. He's at home, slowly unwrapping his layers of black prophet clothes. He is very sick and sad.*

MORMON MOTHER. I smell a salt wind.

HARPER. From the ocean.

MORMON MOTHER. Means he's coming back. Then you'll know. Then you'll eat fire. (*Singing.*) 'Bring back, bring back, oh bring back my bonnie to me, to me . . . '

HARPER (*joining in*). 'Bring back, bring back, oh bring back my bonnie to me.'

> *As they sing,* LOUIS *leaves* JOE *alone at the beach. Back in Manhattan, he goes to a streetside payphone, dials a number.* PRIOR *is alone in his bedroom. He is taking his medication. The phone rings in his apartment. He picks it up.*

PRIOR. Wait, I have a mouthful of pills and water, I . . .

LOUIS. Prior? It's Lou.

> PRIOR *swallows.*

LOUIS. I want to see you.

ACT FOUR: John Brown's Body   February 1986

Scene One

A day later. Split Scene: LOUIS *sitting, cold, on a park bench.*
ROY *and* JOE *in* ROY's *hospital room.* ROY's *in bed, hooked up
as usual to an IV drip. His condition has worsened.* JOE *sits in a
chair nearby.*

ROY. If you want the smoke and puffery you can listen to
Kissinger and Schultz and those guys, but if you want to look at
the heart of modern conservatism, you look at me. Everyone
else has abandoned the struggle, everything nowadays is just
sipping tea with Nixon and Mao, that was *disgusting*, did you
see that? Were you born yet?

JOE. Of course I . . .

ROY. My generation, we had *clarity*. Unafraid to look deep into
the miasma at the heart of the world, what a pit, what a
nightmare is there – *I* have looked, I have searched all my life
for absolute bottom, and I found it, *believe* me: *Stygian*. How
tragic, how brutal and short life is. How sinful people are. The
immutable heart of what we are that bleeds through whatever
we might become. All else is vanity.
  I don't know the world anymore.

He coughs.

After I die they'll say it was for the money and the headlines.
But it was never the money: it's the moxie that counts. I never
wavered. You: remember.

JOE. I will, Roy.
  I was afraid you wouldn't want to see me. If you'd forgive
me. For letting you down.

ROY. Forgiveness.
  You seen a lady around here, dumpy lady, stupid . . . hat?
She . . . Oh boy. Oh boy, no she's off watching the hearings.
Treacherous bitch.

JOE. Who?

ROY. Did you get a blessing from your father before he died?

JOE. A blessing?

ROY. Yeah.

JOE. No.

ROY. He should have done that. Life. That's what they're supposed to bless. Life.

ROY motions for JOE to come over, then for him to kneel. He puts his hand on JOE's forehead. JOE leans the weight of his head into ROY's hand. They both close their eyes and enjoy it for a moment.

JOE (*quietly*). Roy, I . . . I need to talk to you about . . .

ROY. Ssshah. Schmendrick. Don't fuck up the magic.

(*He removes his hand.*) A *Brokhe*. You don't even have to trick it out of me, like what's-his-name in the Bible.

JOE. Jacob.

ROY. That's the one. A ruthless motherfucker, some bald runt, but he laid hold of his birthright with his claws and his teeth. Jacob's father – what was the guy's name?

JOE. Isaac.

ROY. Yeah. The sacrifice. That jerk.
    My mother read me those stories.
    See this scar on my nose? When I was three months old, there was a bony spur, she made them operate, shave it off. They said I was too young for surgery, I'd outgrow it but she insisted. I figure she wanted to toughen me up. And it worked. I am tough. It's taking a lot . . . to dismantle me.

PRIOR enters and sits on the bench, as far as he can from LOUIS.

PRIOR. Oh this is going to be so much worse than I'd imagined.

LOUIS. Hello.

PRIOR. Fuck you you little shitbag.

LOUIS. Don't waste energy beating up on me, OK? I'm already taking care of that.

PRIOR. Don't see any bruises.

LOUIS. Inside.

PRIOR. You are one noble guy. Inside. Don't flatter yourself, Louis. So. It's your tea-party. Talk.

LOUIS. It's good to see you again. I missed you.

PRIOR. Talk.

LOUIS. I want to . . . try to make up.

PRIOR. Make up.

LOUIS. Yes. But . . .

PRIOR. Aha. But.

LOUIS. But you don't have to be so hostile. Don't I get any points for trying to arrive at a resolution? Maybe what I did isn't forgivable but . . .

PRIOR. It isn't.

LOUIS. But. I'm trying to be responsible. Prior. There are limits. Boundaries. And you have to be reasonable.
    Why are you dressed like that?

Little pause.

PRIOR. You were saying something about being reasonable.

LOUIS. I've been giving this a lot of thought. Yes I fucked up, that's obvious. But maybe you fucked up too. You never trusted me, you never gave me a chance to find my footing, not really, you were so quick to attack and . . . I think, maybe just too much of a victim, finally. Passive. Dependent. And what I think is that people do have a choice about how they handle . . .

PRIOR. You want to come back. Why?

LOUIS. I didn't say I wanted to come back.

Pause.

PRIOR. Oh.
    No, you didn't.

LOUIS (*softly, almost pleading*). I can't. Move in again, start all over again. I don't think it'd be any different.

Little pause.

PRIOR. You're seeing someone else.

LOUIS (*shocked*). What? No.

PRIOR. You are.

LOUIS. I'M NOT. Well, occasionally a . . . he's a . . . just a pick up, how do you . . .

PRIOR. Threshold of revelation. Now: Ask me how I know he's a Mormon.

Pause. LOUIS stares.

PRIOR. *Is* he a Mormon?

Little pause.

    Well, goddamn. Ask me how I knew.

LOUIS. How?

PRIOR. Fuck you. I'm a prophet.

(*Furious.*) *Reasonable? Limits?* Tell it to my *lungs*, stupid, tell it to my lesions, tell it to the cotton-woolly patches in my eyes!

LOUIS. Prior, I . . . haven't seen him for days now . . .

PRIOR. I'm going, I have limits too.

PRIOR starts to leave. He has an attack of some sort of respiratory trouble. He sits heavily on the bench. LOUIS starts to go near him, PRIOR waves him away. PRIOR looks at LOUIS.

You cry, but you endanger nothing in yourself. It's like the idea of crying when you do it.
   Or the idea of love.

ROY. Now you have to go.

JOE. I left my wife.

Little pause.

I needed to tell you.

ROY. It happens.

JOE. I've been staying with someone. Else. For a whole month now.

ROY. It happens.

JOE. With a . . . man.

Pause.

ROY. A man?

JOE. Yes.

ROY. You're with a man?

JOE. Yes I . . .

ROY sits up in his bed. He puts his legs over the side, away from where JOE is sitting.

ROY. I gotta . . .

JOE. You . . . what, the . . . um, bathroom or . . .

ROY stands, unsteadily. he starts to walk away from the bed. The IV tube in his arm extends to its full length and then pulls. ROY looks down at it, remembering it's there. In a calm, even disinterested manner he pulls it out of his arm.

ROY. Ow.

JOE. Roy, what are you . . .

JOE *starts for the door,* ROY *stands still watching dark blood run down his arm.*

JOE (*calling off*). Um, help, please, I think he . . .

BELIZE *enters with the portable oxygen, and then sees* ROY.

BELIZE. Holy shit.

BELIZE *puts on rubber gloves, starts towards* ROY.

ROY. Get the fuck away from me.

JOE (*going towards* ROY). Roy, please, get back into . . .

ROY. SHUT UP!
    Now you listen to me.

JOE *nods.*

BELIZE. Get your . . .

ROY. SHUT UP I SAID.

(*To* JOE.) I want you home. With your wife. Whatever else you got going, cut it dead.

JOE. I can't, Roy, I need to be with . . .

ROY *grabs* JOE *by the shirt, smearing it with blood.*

ROY. YOU NEED? Listen to me. Do what I say. Or you will regret it. And don't talk to me about it. *Ever again.*

BELIZE *moves in, takes* ROY *to the bed and starts bandaging the puncture.*

ROY. I . . . never saw that coming. You kill me.

BELIZE (*to* JOE). Get somewhere you can take off that shirt and throw it out, and don't touch the blood.

JOE. Why? I don't unders . . .

ROY. OUT! OUT! You already got my blessing – WHAT MORE DO YOU WANT FROM ME?

He has a terrible wracking spasm.

BELIZE (*to* JOE). Get the fuck outa here.

JOE. I . . . Roy, please I . . .

ROY (*exhausted*). You what, you want to stay and watch *this*? Well fuck you too.

JOE *leaves.* BELIZE *finishes bandaging.*

PRIOR. So. Your new lover . . .

LOUIS. He's not my . . .

PRIOR. Tell me where you met him.

LOUIS. In the park. Well, first at work, he . . .

PRIOR. He's a lawyer or a judge?

LOUIS. Lawyer.

PRIOR. A Gay Mormon lawyer.

LOUIS. Yes. Republican too.

PRIOR. A Gay Mormon Republican Lawyer. (*With contempt.*)
Louis . . .

LOUIS. But he's sort of, I don't know if the word would be . . .
well, in a way sensitive, and I . . .

PRIOR. Ah. A *sensitive* gay Republican.

LOUIS. He's just company. Companionship.

Pause.

PRIOR. Companionship. Oh.
   You know just when I think he couldn't possibly say any-
thing to make it worse, he does. Companionship. How *good*.
I wouldn't want you to be *lonely*.
   There are thousands of gay men in New York City with
AIDS and nearly every one of them is being taken care of by . .
. a friend or by . . . a lover who has stuck by them through
things worse than my . . . So far. Everyone got that, except me.
I got you. Why? What's wrong with me?

LOUIS *is crying.*

Louis?
   Are you really bruised inside?

LOUIS. I can't have this talk anymore.

PRIOR. Oh the list of things you can't do. So fragile! Answer me:
Inside: Bruises?

LOUIS. Yes.

PRIOR. Come back to me when they're visible. I want to see black
and blue, Louis, I want to see blood. Because I can't believe
you even *have* blood in your veins till you show it to me. So
don't come near me again, unless you've got something to
show. (*Exits.*)

ROY (*looking at the door through which* JOE *exited*). Every
goddam thing I ever wanted they have taken from me. Mocked
and reviled, all my life.

BELIZE. Join the club.

ROY. I don't belong to any club you could get through the front door of.

> You watch yourself you take too many liberties.
> What's your name?

BELIZE (*a beat, then*). Norman Arriaga. Belize to my friends, but you can call me Norman Arriaga.

ROY. Tell me something, Norman, you ever hire a lawyer?

BELIZE. No Roy. Never did.

ROY. Hire a lawyer, sue somebody, it's good for the soul.

> Lawyers are . . . the High Priests of America. We alone know the words that made America. Out of thin air. We alone know how to use The Words. The Law: the only club I ever wanted to belong to. And before they take that from me, I'm going to die.

> ROY *has a series of terrible spasms, which shake him violently.* BELIZE *approaches.* ROY *grabs* BELIZE *by both arms.* BELIZE *tries to pull away, but* ROY *hangs on, shaking them both. During this seizure,* ETHEL *appears.*

ROY. Sssshhh. Fire. Out. (*It isn't. Violent spasms continue.*) God have mercy. This is a lousy way to go.

BELIZE. God have mercy.

ROY (*seeing* ETHEL). Look who's back.

BELIZE (*looking around, seeing no one*). Who?

ROY. Mrs. Reddy Kilowatt.

> Fucking horror. How's . . . Yonkers?

BELIZE. I almost feel sorry for you.

ETHEL. A bad idea.

ROY. Yeah. Pity. Repulsive.

> (*To* BELIZE.) You. Me. (*He snaps his fingers.*) No. Connection. Nobody . . . with me now. But the dead.

Scene Two

The next day. JOE *in his office at the Hall of Justice in Brooklyn. He sits at his desk dejectedly, head in hands.* PRIOR *and* BELIZE *enter the corridor outside.*

PRIOR (*whisper*). That's his office.

BELIZE (*whisper*). This is stupid.

PRIOR (*whisper*). Go home if you're chicken.

BELIZE. *You're* the one who should be home.

PRIOR. I have a hobby now: haunting people. Fuck home. You wait here. I want to meet my replacement.

He goes to JOE's *door, steps in.*

PRIOR. Oh.

JOE. Yes, can I . . .

PRIOR. You look just like the dummy. She's right.

JOE. Who's right?

PRIOR. Your wife.

Pause.

JOE. What?
    Do you know my . . .

PRIOR. No.

JOE. You said my wife.

PRIOR. No I didn't.

JOE. Yes you did.

PRIOR. You misheard. I'm a Prophet.

JOE. What?

PRIOR. PROPHET PROPHET I PROPHESY I HAVE SIGHT I *SEE*.
    What do *you* do?

JOE. I'm a clerk.

PRIOR. Oh big deal. A clerk. You *what*, you file things? Well you better be keeping a file on the hearts you break, that's all that counts in the end, you'll have bills to pay in the world to come, you and your friend, the Whore of Babylon.

Pause.

Sorry wrong room.

Exits, goes to BELIZE.

(*Despairing.*) He's the Marlboro Man.

BELIZE. Oooh, I wanna see.

BELIZE *goes to* JOE's *office.* JOE *is standing, perplexed.* BELIZE *sees* JOE *and instantly recognizes him.*

BELIZE. *SACRED* Heart of Jesus!

JOE. Now what is . . .
     You're Roy's nurse. I recognize you, you're . . .

BELIZE. No you don't.

JOE. From the hospital. You're Roy Cohn's nurse.

BELIZE. No I'm not. Not a nurse. We all look alike to you. You
     all look alike to us. It's a mad mad world. Have a nice day.

Exits, back to PRIOR.

PRIOR. Home on the range?

BELIZE. Chaps and spurs. Now girl we *got* to get you home and
     into . . .

PRIOR. Mega-butch. He made me feel beyond nelly. Like little
     wispy daisies were sprouting out my ears. Little droopy wispy
     wilted . . .

JOE *comes out of his office.*

BELIZE. Run! Run!

JOE. Wait!

They're cornered by JOE. BELIZE *keeps his face averted and
partially hidden by his scarf.*

JOE. What game are you playing, this is a federal courthouse. You
     said . . . something about my wife. Now what . . . How do you
     know my . . .

PRIOR. I'm . . . Nothing. I'm a mental patient. He's my nurse.

BELIZE. Not his nurse, I'm not a n . . .

PRIOR. We're here because my will is being contested. Um, what
     is that called, when they challenge your will?

JOE. Competency? But this is an appellate court.

PRIOR. And I am appealing to anyone, anyone in the universe,
     who will listen to me for some . . . Charity . . . Some people are
     so greedy, such pigs, they have everything, health, everything,
     and still they want more.

JOE. You said my wife. And I want to know, is she . . .

PRIOR. TALK TO HER YOURSELF, BULLWINKLE! WHAT
     DO I LOOK LIKE A MARRIAGE COUNSELLOR?
     Oh nursey dear, fetch the medication, I'm starting to rave.

BELIZE. Pardons, Monsieur L'Avocat, nous sommes absolument
     Desolée.

PRIOR *blows a raspberry at* JOE.

BELIZE. Behave yourself, chérie, or nanny will have to use the wooden spoon.

PRIOR *exits.*

BELIZE (*to* JOE, *dropping scarf disguise*). I am trapped in a world of white people. That's *my* problem.

Exits.

Scene Three

The next day. A stormy cold late-February day. At the Bethesda Fountain in Central Park. It's drizzling. LOUIS *is sitting on a bench in the tunnel that looks out on the fountain.* BELIZE *enters with an umbrella; as he approaches the bench he shakes the umbrella, showering* LOUIS, *then closes it and sits.*

BELIZE. Nice angel.

LOUIS. What angel?

BELIZE. The fountain.

LOUIS (*looking*). Bethesda.

BELIZE. What's she commemorate? Louis, I'll bet you know.

LOUIS. Naval dead of the Civil War.

BELIZE. The Civil War. I knew you'd know. You are nothing if not well informed.

LOUIS. This is Prior's favourite place in the park.
        Listen I saw him yesterday. Prior.

BELIZE. Prior is *upset.*

LOUIS. Is he OK? He seemed . . . well not himself, he seemed . . .

BELIZE. Crazy?

LOUIS. Is he having . . . is he delusional, or . . .

BELIZE. With a little help from his friends.

LOUIS. Listen, this guy I'm seeing, I'm not seeing him now. Prior misunderstood, he jumped to . . .

BELIZE. Oh yeah. Your new beau. Prior and me, we went to the courthouse. Scoped him out.

LOUIS. *You had no right to do that.*

BELIZE. Oh did we violate your *rights*. What did you drag me out here for, Louis, I don't have *time* for you. You walk out on your lover. Days don't pass before you are out on the town with somebody new. But *this* . . .

LOUIS. I'm *not* out on the . . . I want you to tell Prior that I . . .

BELIZE. *This* is a record low: sharing your dank and dirty bed with Roy Cohn's buttboy.

Pause.

LOUIS. Come again?

BELIZE. Doesn't that bother you at all?

LOUIS. *Roy Cohn*? What the fuck are you . . . I am not sharing my bed with Roy Cohn's . . .

BELIZE. Your little friend didn't tell you, huh? You and Hoss Cartwright, it's not a verbal kind of thing, you just kick off your boots and hit the hay.

LOUIS. Joe Pitt is not Roy Cohn's . . . Joe is a very moral man, he's not even *that* conservative, or . . . well not that *kind* of a . . . And I don't want to continue this.

BELIZE (*starting to go*). Bye bye.

LOUIS. It's not my fault that Prior left you for me.

BELIZE. I beg your pardon.

LOUIS. You have always hated me. Because you are in love with Prior and you were when I met him and he fell in love with me, and so now you cook up this . . . I mean how do you know this? That Joe and *Roy Cohn* are . . .

BELIZE. I don't know whether Mr. Cohn has penetrated more than his spiritual sphincter. All I'm saying is you better hope there's no GOP germ, Louis, 'cause if there is, you got it.

LOUIS. *I don't believe you*. Not *Roy Cohn*. He's like the polestar of human evil, he's like the worst human being who ever lived, he isn't *human* even, he's . . . You think everything is black and white, good and evil, just because somebody is a Republican they're in bed with Roy Cohn. People like you finally fail to have an adequately grown-up, nuanced view of the world, you're Manichean, Joe is . . . well, sort of past ideology, not just another lost ineffectual leftie like me, moaning all the time about history and guilt, because this is a new era, you know, things are different now, uglier, scarier, I mean the rest of us should just surrender, just surrender, just give the fuck up, I mean. . . . *Oh God. I am so fucking wet and miserable.*

BELIZE. Finished?

LOUIS. And he . . . . And . . .

BELIZE. And he's a clerk for a Republican federal judge.
    You know what your problem is, Louis? Your problem is
that you are so full of piping hot crap that the mention of your
name draws flies.
    Just so's the record's straight: I love Prior but I was never in
love with him. I have a man, uptown, and I have since *long*
before I first laid my eyes on the sorry-ass sight of you.

LOUIS. I . . . I didn't know that you . . .

BELIZE. No 'cause you never bothered to ask.
    Up in the air, just like that angel, too far off the earth to pick
out the details. Louis and his Big Ideas. Big ideas are all you
love. 'America' is what Louis loves.

Little pause.

LOUIS. So what? Maybe I do. You don't know what I love. You
don't.

BELIZE. Well I hate America, Louis. I hate this country. It's
just big ideas, and stories, and people dying, and people like
you.
    The white cracker who wrote the National Anthem knew
what he was doing. He set the word 'free' to a note so high
nobody can reach it. That was deliberate. Nothing on earth
sounds less like freedom to me.
    You come with me to room 1013 over at the hospital, I'll
show you America. Terminal, crazy and mean.

A rumble of thunder.

I *live* in America, Louis, that's hard enough, I don't have to
love it. You do that. Everybody's got to love something.

LOUIS. Everybody does.

Scene Four

Same day. HANNAH *at the Visitors' Centre.* JOE *enters. They
look at each other for a long moment.*

JOE. How is she?

HANNAH. Nothing surprising.

JOE. Is she OK?

HANNAH. Well *that* would be surprising. Wouldn't it?

Can I . . .

JOE. There is no possible thing I can imagine you doing. Ma. You shouldn't have come.

HANNAH. You already made that clear as day. For a month now. You can't even return a simple phone call.

JOE. A phone call from you . . . is not so simple.

HANNAH. Just so I would have something to tell her. You've been living on some rainy rooftop for all we knew. It's cruel.

JOE. Not intended to be.

HANNAH. You're sure about that.

JOE (*a beat, then*). I'm taking her home.

HANNAH. You think that's best for her, you think that she . . .

JOE. I . . . know what I'm doing.

HANNAH. I don't think you have a clue. Which is only typical of you. You're a man, you botch up, it's not such a big deal, but she . . .

JOE. Just being a man doesn't . . .

HANNAH. Being a woman's harder. Look at her.

JOE (*a beat, then, softly*). It's a big deal, Ma, botching up. I could use some . . .

HANNAH. Sympathy?

Little pause.

If I could manage any, you'd just push it away. You want sympathy? Then why'd you come here?

JOE. I migrated across the breadth of the continent of North America, I ran all this way to get away from . . . (*He stops.*) Is she . . . ?

HANNAH. She's not here.

JOE. But . . . she's not at the apartment, I . . .

HANNAH (*a beat, then*). Then she escaped. Good for her.
Ask yourself what it was you were running from. It's time you did. Not from me, I was nothing. From what? And what are you running from now?

JOE. You and me. It's like we're back in Salt Lake again. You sort of bring the desert with you.

Little pause.

Are you . . . Don't cry.

HANNAH. If I ever do. I promise you you'll not be privileged to witness it.

JOE. It was a mistake. I should never have called you. Ma. You should never have come. I can't imagine why you did.

JOE exits. HANNAH sits.

PRIOR enters.

PRIOR. That man who was just here.

HANNAH (*not looking at him*). We're closed. Go away.

PRIOR. He's your son.

HANNAH looks at PRIOR. Little pause. PRIOR turns to leave.

HANNAH. Do you know him. That man?

Little pause.

How do you know that . . .

PRIOR. My ex-boyfriend, he knows him, *now* – I wanted to warn your son about *later*, when his hair goes and there's hips and jowls and all that . . . human stuff, that poor slob there's just gonna wind up miserable, fat, frightened and *alone* because Louis, he can't handle bodies.

HANNAH (*a beat, then*). Are you a . . . a homosexual?

PRIOR. Oh is it *that* obvious? Yes. I am. What's it to you?

HANNAH. Would you say you are a typical . . . homosexual?

PRIOR. Me? Oh I'm *stereotypical*. What, you mean like am I a hairdresser or . . .

HANNAH. Are you a hairdresser?

PRIOR. Well it would be *your* lucky day if I was because frankly . . .

I'm sick. I'm sick. It's expensive.

He starts to cry.

Oh shit now I won't be able to stop, now it's started. I feel really terrible, do I have a fever?

(*Offering his forehead, impatiently.*) Do I have a fever?

She hesitates, then puts her hand on his forehead.

HANNAH. Yes.

PRIOR. How high?

HANNAH. There might be a thermometer in the . . .

PRIOR. Very high, very high, could you get me to a cab, I think

I want . . . (*He sits heavily on the floor.*) Don't be alarmed, it's worse than it looks, I mean . . .

HANNAH. You should . . . Try to stand up, or . . . let me see if anyone can . . .

PRIOR (*listening to his lungs*). Sssshhh.
      Echo-breath, it's . . . (*He shakes his head 'No good'.*) I . . . overdid it. I'm in trouble again.
      Take me to St. Vincent's Hospital, I mean, help me to a cab to the . . .

Little pause, then HANNAH *exits and reenters with her coat on.*

HANNAH. Can you stand up?

PRIOR. You don't . . . Call me a . . .

HANNAH. I'm useless here.

She helps him stand.

PRIOR. Please, if you're trying to convert me this isn't a good time.

Distant thunder.

HANNAH. Lord, look at it out there. It's pitch-black.
      Storm's coming in. We better move.

They exit. Thunder.

Scene Five

Same day, late afternoon. HARPER *is standing in an icy wind at the railing of the Promenade in Brooklyn Heights, staring at the river and the Manhattan skyline. The rain is falling. She is wearing a dress, inadequate for the weather, and she's barefoot.* JOE *enters with an umbrella. They stare at each other. Then* HARPER *turns to face the skyline.*

HARPER. The end of the world is at hand. Hello, paleface.
      Nothing like storm clouds over Manhattan to get you in the mood for Judgement Day.

Thunder.

JOE. It's freezing, it's starting to rain, where are your shoes?

HARPER. I threw them in the river.
      The Judgement Day. Everyone will think they're crazy now,

not just me, everyone will see things. Sick men will see angels, women who *have* houses will sell their houses, dimestore dummies will rear up on their wood-putty legs and roam the land, looking for brides.

JOE. Let's go home.

HARPER. Where's that?
    (*Pointing towards Manhattan.*) Want to buy an island? It's going out of business. You can have it for the usual cheap trinkets. Fire sale. The prices are insane.

JOE. Harper.

HARPER. Joe.

A beat.

Did you miss me?

JOE. I . . . I've come back.

HARPER. Oh I know.
    Here's why I wanted to stay in Brooklyn. The Promenade view. Water won't ever accomplish the end. No matter how much you cry. Flood's not the answer, people just float.
    Let's go home.
    Fire's the answer. The Great and Terrible Day. At last.

Scene Six

Night. PRIOR, EMILY *and* HANNAH *in an examination room in St. Vincent's Emergency Room.* EMILY *is listening to* PRIOR's *breathing, while* HANNAH *sits in a nearby chair.*

EMILY. You've lost eight pounds. Eight pounds! I know people who would kill to be in the shape you were in, you were *recovering*, and you threw it away.

PRIOR. This isn't about WEIGHT, it's about LUNGS, UM . . . PNEUMONIA.

EMILY. We don't know yet.

PRIOR. THE FUCK WE DON'T ASSHOLE YOU MAY NOT BUT I *CAN'T BREATHE.*

HANNAH. You'd breathe better if you didn't holler like that.

PRIOR (*looks at* HANNAH, *then*). This is my ex-lover's lover's Mormon mother.

Little pause.

EMILY. Even in New York in the Eighties, *that* is strange. Keep breathing. Stop moving. STAY PUT.

She exits.

HANNAH (*standing to go*). I should go.

PRIOR. I'm not insane.

HANNAH. I didn't say you . . .

PRIOR. I saw an angel. That's insane.

HANNAH. Well, it's . . .

PRIOR. Insane. But I'm not insane. But then why did I do this to myself? Because I have been driven insane by . . . your son and by that lying . . . Because ever since She arrived, ever since, I have been consumed by this ice-cold, razorblade terror that just shouts and shouts 'Keep moving! Run!' And I've run myself . . . Into the ground. Right where She said I'd eventually be. She seemed so real. What's happened to me?

Little pause.

HANNAH. You had a vision.

PRIOR. A vision. Thank you, Maria Ouspenskaya.
    I'm not so far gone I can be assuaged by pity and lies.

HANNAH. I don't have pity. It's just not something I have.

Little pause.

One hundred and seventy years ago, which is recent, an angel of God appeared to Joseph Smith in upstate New York, not far from here. People have visions.

PRIOR. But that's preposterous, that's . . .

HANNAH. It's not polite to call other people's beliefs preposterous. He had great need of understanding. Our Prophet. His desire made prayer. His prayer made an angel. The angel was real. I believe that.

PRIOR. I don't. And I'm sorry but it's repellent to me. So much of what you believe.

HANNAH. What do I believe?

PRIOR. I'm a homosexual. With AIDS. I can just imagine what you . . .

HANNAH. No you can't. Imagine. The things in my head. You don't make assumptions about me, mister; I won't make them about you.

PRIOR (*a beat; he looks at her, then*). Fair enough.

HANNAH. My son is . . . well, like you.

PRIOR. Homosexual.

HANNAH (*a nod, then*). I flew into a rage when he told me, mad as hornets. At first I assumed it was about his . . .

She shrugs.

PRIOR. Homosexuality.

HANNAH. But that wasn't it. Homosexuality. It just seems . . . ungainly. Two men together. It isn't an appetizing notion but then, for me, men in *any* configuration . . . well they're so lumpish and stupid. And stupidity gets me cross.

PRIOR. I wish you would be more true to your demographic profile. Life is confusing enough.

Little pause. They look at each other.

PRIOR. You know the Bible, you know . . .

HANNAH. Reasonably well, I . . .

PRIOR. The prophets in the Bible, do they . . . ever refuse their vision?

HANNAH. There's scriptural precedent, yes.

PRIOR. And what does God do to them? When they do that?

HANNAH. He . . . Well, he feeds them to whales.

They both laugh. PRIOR's laugh brings on breathing trouble.

HANNAH. Just lie still. You'll be alright.

PRIOR. No. I won't be. My lungs are getting tighter. The fever mounts and you get delirious. And then days of delirium and awful pain and drugs; you start slipping and then.
    I really . . . fucked up. I'm scared. I can't do it again.

HANNAH. You shouldn't talk that way. You ought to make a better show of yourself.

PRIOR. Look at this . . . horror.

He shows her a lesion, the same one on his arm he showed LOUIS in Act One of Millennium. *Then he pulls up his shirt, revealing more.*

See? That's not human. That's why I run. Wouldn't you?

Wouldn't anybody.

HANNAH. It's a cancer. Nothing more. Nothing more human than that.

PRIOR. Oh God, I want to be done.

(To heaven.) I want to be done.

HANNAH. An angel is just a belief, with wings and arms that can carry you. It's naught to be afraid of. If it lets you down, reject it. Seek for something new.

PRIOR. I . . .

He stirs uncomfortably, adjusts his lap.

PRIOR. Oh my.

HANNAH. What?

PRIOR. Listen.

Distant thunder.

PRIOR. It's Her. Oh my God.

HANNAH. It's the spring rain is all.

PRIOR. No. She's coming for me now. She said she would.
     Stay with me.

HANNAH. Oh no, I . . .

PRIOR. You comfort me, you do, you stiffen my spine.

HANNAH. When I got up this morning this is not how I envisioned the day would end.
     I'm not needed elsewhere.

PRIOR. If I sleep, will you keep watch?
     She's approaching.

HANNAH. She is?

PRIOR *(nodding his head yes)*. Modesty forbids my explaining exactly *how* I know, but I have an infallible barometer of her proximity.
     And it's rising.

Scene Seven

That night. HARPER and JOE at home, in bed. A silence, then:

HARPER. When we have sex. Why do you keep your eyes closed?

JOE. I don't.

HARPER. You always do. You can say why, I already know the answer.

JOE. Then why do I have to . . .

HARPER. You imagine things.
Imagine men.

JOE. Yes.

HARPER. Imagining, just like me, except the only time I wasn't imagining was when I was with you. You, the one part of the real world I wasn't allergic to.

JOE. Please. Don't.

HARPER. But I only *thought* I wasn't dreaming.

JOE sits up abruptly, turns his back to her. Then he starts to put on his pants.

HARPER. Oh. Oh. Back in Brooklyn, back with . . .

JOE (*not looking at her*). I'm going out. I have to get some stuff I left behind.

HARPER. Look at me.

He doesn't. He keeps dressing.

HARPER. Look at me.

Look at me.

(*Loud.*) HERE! LOOK HERE AT . . .

JOE (*looking at her*). *What?*

HARPER. What do you see?

JOE. What do I . . . ?

HARPER. What do you see?

JOE. *Nothing*, I . . .

Little pause.

HARPER. Thank you.

JOE. For what?

HARPER. The truth.

JOE (*a beat, then*). I'm going. Out. Just . . . Out.

He exits.

HARPER. Goodbye.

Scene Eight

Later that night. LOUIS *in his apartment. He has a thick file full of xeroxed articles. He is reading.* JOE *enters. They stare at each other.*

LOUIS. Have you no decency, sir? At long last? Have you no sense of decency?
    Who said that?

JOE. Who said . . . ?

LOUIS. Who said, 'Have you no . . . '

JOE. I don't . . . I've come back.
    Please let me in.

LOUIS. You're in.

JOE. I'm having a very hard time, Louis.
    It's so good to see you again.

LOUIS. You *really* don't know who said, 'Have you no decency?'

JOE. What's wrong? Why are you . . .

LOUIS. OK, second question: *Have* you no decency?
    Guess what I spent the rainy afternoon doing?

JOE. What?

LOUIS. My homework. Research at the Courthouse. Look what I got: The Decisions of Judge Theodore Wilson, Second Circuit Court of Appeals. 1981-1984. The Reagan Years.

JOE. You, um, you read my decisions.

Little pause.

LOUIS. *Your* decisions. Yes.
    The librarian was gay, he had all the good dish, he told me that Wilson didn't write these opinions any more than Nixon wrote *Six Crises* . . .

JOE. Or Kennedy wrote *Profiles in Courage*.

LOUIS. Or Reagan wrote *Where's the Rest of Me*? Or you and I wrote the Book Of Love.

JOE (*trying to soothe things, going to* LOUIS). Listen, I don't want to do this now. I mean it, I need you to stop attacking and . . .

LOUIS *shoves* JOE *away, hard.*

JOE. Hey!

LOUIS. These gems were ghostwritten. By you: His obedient clerk. Naturally I was eager to read them.

JOE. Free country.

LOUIS. Uh-huh. I love the one where you found against those women on Staten Island who were suing the New Jersey factory, the toothpaste-makers whose orange-coloured smoke was *blinding children* . . .

JOE. Not blind, just minor irritation.

LOUIS. Three of them had to be *hospitalized. Joe.* It's sort of brilliant, in a satanic sort of way, how you conclude that these women have no right to sue under the Air and Water Protection Act because the Air and Water Protection Act doesn't protect *people*, but actually only *air and water*! Amazing!
(*Flipping through the cases.*) Have you no decency, have you no . . .

JOE. I don't believe this. My opinions are being criticized by the guy who changes the coffee filters in the secretaries' lounge!

LOUIS. But my *absolute favourite* is this:
Stephens versus the United States: The army guy who got a dishonourable discharge – for being gay. Now as I understand it, this Stephens had told the army he was gay when he enlisted, but when he got ready to retire they booted him out. Cheat the queer of his pension.

JOE. Right. And he sued. And he won the case. He got the pension back. So what are you . . .

LOUIS. The first judges gave him his pension back, *yes*, because: they ruled that gay men are members of a legitimate minority, entitled to the special protection of the Fourteenth Amendment of the US Constitution. Equal Protection under the Law.
I can just imagine how the news of that momentary lapse into decency was received. So then all the judges on the Second Circuit were assembled, and . . .

JOE. We found for the guy again.

LOUIS. But but but!
On an equitable estoppel. I had to look that up, I'm Mr. Coffee, I can't be expected to know these things.
They didn't change the *decision*, they just changed the *reason for* the decision. Right? They gave it to him on a technicality: The army knew Stephens was gay when he enlisted. That's all, that's why he won. Not because it's

unconstitutional to discriminate against homosexuals. Because homosexuals, they write, are *not* entitled to equal protection under the law.

JOE. You're being really melodramatic, as usual, you . . .

LOUIS. Actually *they* didn't write this. You did. They gave this opinion to Wilson to write, which since they *know* he's a vegetable incapable of writing do-re-mi, was quite the vote of confidence in his industrious little clerk. This is an important bit of legal fag-bashing, isn't it? They trusted you to do it. And you didn't disappoint.

JOE. It's law not justice, it's power, not the merits of its exercise, it's not an expression of the ideal, it's . . .

LOUIS. So who said, 'Have you no decency?'

JOE. I'm leaving.

LOUIS. You moron, how can you not know that?

JOE (*overlapping*). I'm leaving, you . . . son of a bitch, get out of my . . .

LOUIS. It's only the greatest punchline in American history.

JOE. Out of my way, Louis.

LOUIS. *'Have you no decency, at long last, sir, have you no decency at all?'*

JOE. I DON'T KNOW WHO SAID IT! WHY ARE YOU DOING THIS TO ME! *I LOVE YOU. I LOVE YOU.* WHY . . .

LOUIS. JOSEPH WELCH, THE ARMY/MCCARTHY HEARINGS. Ask ROY. He'll tell you. He knows. He was *there*.
      Roy Cohn. What I want to know is, did you fuck him?

JOE. Did I what?

LOUIS. How often has the latex-sheathed cock I put in my mouth been previously in the mouth of the most evil, twisted, vicious bastard ever to snort coke at Studio 54, because lips that kissed those lips will never kiss mine.

JOE. Don't worry about that, just get out of the . . .

JOE *tries to push* LOUIS *aside;* LOUIS *pushes back, forcefully.*

LOUIS. Did you fuck him, did he pay you to let him . . .

JOE. MOVE!

LOUIS *throws the xeroxes in* JOE's *face. They fly everywhere.* JOE *pushes* LOUIS, LOUIS *grabs* JOE.

LOUIS. You *lied* to me, you *love* me, well fuck you, you cheap piece of . . .

JOE *slugs* LOUIS *in the stomach, hard.* LOUIS *goes to his knees. Then starts to stand up again, badly winded.*

LOUIS. He's got AIDS! Did you even *know* that? Stupid closeted bigots, you probably never figured out that each other was . . .

JOE. Shut up. (*He punches* LOUIS *again.*)

LOUIS. Fascist hypocrite lying filthy . . .

LOUIS *tries to hit* JOE, *and* JOE *starts to hit* LOUIS *repeatedly.* LOUIS *clings to* JOE *as he punches away.*

LOUIS. Oh jeeesus, aw jeez, oh . . .

LOUIS *falls to the floor.* JOE *stands over him.*

JOE. Now stop . . . Now stop . . . I . . .
Please. Say you're OK, please. *Please.*

LOUIS (*not moving*). That . . . Hurt.

JOE. I never did that before, I never hit anyone before, I . . .

LOUIS *sits up. His mouth and eye have been cut.*

JOE. Can you open it? Can you see?

LOUIS. I can see blood.

JOE. Let me get a towel, let me . . .

LOUIS (*pushing* JOE *away*). I could have you arrested you . . .
Creep. They'd think I put you in jail for beating me up.

JOE. I never hit anyone before, I . . .

LOUIS. But it'd really be for those decisions.
It was like a sex scene in an Ayn Rand novel, huh?

JOE. I hurt you. I'm sorry, Louis, I never hit anyone before, I . . .

LOUIS. Yeah yeah get lost. Before I really lose my temper and hurt you back.
I just want to lie here and bleed for a while. Do me good.

Scene Nine

Later that night. ROY *in a very serious hospital bed, monitoring machines and IV drips galore.* ETHEL *appears.*

ROY. John Brown's Body lies a moulderin' in the grave,

John Brown's Body lies a moulderin' in the grave,
John Brown's Body lies a moulderin' in the grave,
His truth is marching on . . .

ETHEL. Look at that big smile. What you got to smile about, Roy?

ROY. I'm going, Ethel. Finally, finally done with this world, at long long last. All mine enemies will be standing on the other shore, mouths gaping open like stupid fish, while the Almighty parts the Sea of Death and lets his Royboy cross over to Jordan. On dry land and still a lawyer.

ETHEL. Don't count your chickens, Roy.
It's over.

ROY. Over?

ETHEL. I wanted the news should come from me.
The panel ruled against you Roy.

ROY. No, no, they only started meeting two days ago.

ETHEL. They recommended disbarment.

ROY. The Executive still has to rule . . . on the recommendation, it'll take another week to sort it out and before then . . .

ETHEL. The Executive was waiting, and they ruled, one two three. They accepted the panel's recommendation.

ROY. I'm . . .

ETHEL. One of the main guys on the Executive leaned over to his friend and said, 'Finally. I've hated that little faggot for thirty-six years.'

ROY. I'm . . . They . . .

ETHEL. They won, Roy. You're not a lawyer anymore.

ROY. But am I dead?

ETHEL. No. They beat you. You lost.

Pause.

I decided to come here so I could see could I forgive you. You who I have hated so terribly I have borne my hatred for you up into the heavens and made a needlesharp little star in the sky out of it. It's the star of Ethel Rosenberg's Hatred, and it burns every year for one night only, June Nineteen. It burns acid green.

I came to forgive but all I can do is take pleasure in your misery. Hoping I'd get to see you die more terrible than I did. And you are, 'cause you're dying in shit, Roy, defeated. And you could kill me, but you couldn't ever defeat me. You never won. And when you die all anyone will say is: better he had never lived at all.

Pause.

ROY. Ma?
  Muddy? Is it . . . ?

(He sits up, looks at ETHEL.) Ma?

ETHEL *(uncertain, then)*. It's Ethel, Roy.

ROY. Muddy? I feel bad.

ETHEL *(looking around)*. Who are you talking to, Roy, it's . . .

ROY. Good to see you, Ma, it's been years.
  I feel bad. Sing to me.

ETHEL. I'm not your mother Roy.

ROY. It's cold in here, I'm up so late, past my time.
  Don't be mad Ma but I'm scared . . . ? A little.
  Don't be mad. Sing me a song. Please.

ETHEL. I don't want to Roy, I'm not your . . .

ROY. Please, it's scary out here. *(He starts to cry.)*

(He sinks back.) Oh God. Oh God, I'm so sorry . . .

ETHEL *(singing, very soft)*.

> Shteit a bocher
> Un er tracht,
> Tracht un tracht
> A gantze nacht:
> Vemen tzu nemen
> Um nit farshemen
> Vemen tsu nemen,
> Um nit farshem.
> Tum-ba-la, Tum-ba-la, Tum-balalaike,
> Tum-ba-la, Tum-ba-la, Tum-balalaike,
> Tum balalaike, Shpil balalaike . . .

Pause.

Roy . . . ? Are you . . . ?

She crosses to the bed, looks at him. Goes back to her chair.

That's it.

BELIZE *enters, goes to the bed.*

BELIZE. Wake up, it's time to . . .

Oh. Oh, you're . . .

ROY *(sitting up violently)*. No I'm NOT!

I fooled you Ethel, I knew who you were all along, I can't believe you fell for that ma stuff, I just wanted to see if I could finally, finally make Ethel Rosenberg sing! I WIN!

He falls back on the bed.

Oh fuck, oh fuck me I . . .
    (*In a very faint voice.*) Next time around: I don't want to be a man. I wanna be an octopus. Remember that, OK? A fucking . . . (*Punching an imaginary button with his finger.*) Hold.

He dies.

ACT FIVE: Heaven, I'm in Heaven   February 1986

Scene One

Very late, same night. PRIOR's *hospital room.* HANNAH *is sleeping in a chair.* PRIOR *is standing on his bed. There's an eerie light on him.* HANNAH *stirs, moans a little, wakes up suddenly, sees him.*

PRIOR. She's on her way.

The lights drain to black.

HANNAH. Turn the lights back on, turn the lights . . .

There is the sound of a silvery trumpet in the dark, and a tattoo of faraway drums. Silence. Thunder. Then all over the walls, Hebrew letters appear, writing in flames. The ANGEL *is there, suddenly. She is dressed in black and looks terrifying.* HANNAH *screams and buries her face in her hands.*

ANGEL. I I I I Have Returned, Prophet,

Thunder.

And not according to Plan.

PRIOR. Take it back.

Big thunderclap.

The Book, whatever you left in me, I won't be its repository, I reject it.

Thunder.

PRIOR (*to* HANNAH). Help me out here. HELP ME!

HANNAH. (*trying to shut it all out*). I don't, I don't, this is a dream it's a dream it's a . . .

PRIOR. I don't think that's really the point right at this particular moment.

HANNAH. I don't know what to . . .

PRIOR (*overlap*). Well it was your idea, reject the vision you said and . . .

HANNAH (*overlap*). Yes but I thought it was more a . . . metaphorical . . . I . . .

PRIOR (*overlap*). You said scriptural precedent, you said . . .
    WHAT AM I SUPPOSED TO . . .

HANNAH (*overlap*). You . . . you . . . wrestle her.

PRIOR. SAY *WHAT*?

HANNAH. It's an angel, you . . . just . . . grab hold and say . . . oh
    what was it, wait, wait, umm . . . OH! Grab her, say 'I will not
    let thee go except thou bless me!' Then wrestle with her till she
    gives in.

PRIOR. YOU wrestle her, I don't know how to wrestle, I . . .

*The ANGEL flies up into the air and lands right in front of
PRIOR. PRIOR grabs her – she emits a terrible, impossibly
loud, shuddering eagle-screech. PRIOR and the ANGEL
wrestle. The wrestling should be in earnest and rapidly become
furious, deadly. As PRIOR gains the upper hand, he begins to
speak.*

PRIOR. I . . . will not let thee go except thou bless me. Take back
    your Book. Anti-Migration, that's so feeble, I can't believe you
    couldn't do better than that, free me, unfetter me, bless me or
    whatever but I will be let go.

ANGEL (*taking to the air, trying to escape; a whole chorus of
    voices*). I I I I Am the CONTINENTAL PRINCIPALITY OF
    AMERICA, I I I I AM THE BIRD OF PREY I Will NOT BE
    COMPELLED, I . . .

*There is a great blast of music and a shaft of white light
streams in through the blue murk. Within this incredibly bright
column of light there is a ladder of even brighter, purer light,
reaching up into infinity. At the conjunctions of each rung there
are flaming alephs.*

ANGEL. Entrance has been gained. Return the Text to Heaven.

PRIOR (*terrified*). Can I come back? I don't want to go unless . . .

ANGEL (*angry*). You have prevailed, Prophet. You . . . Choose.
    Now release me.
    I have torn a muscle in my thigh.

PRIOR. Big deal, my leg's been hurting for months.

*He releases the ANGEL. He hesitates. He ascends. The room is
instantly plunged into near darkness. The ANGEL turns her
attention to HANNAH.*

HANNAH. What? What? You've got no business with me, I didn't
    call you, you're *his* fever dream not mine, and he's gone now
    and you should go too, I'm waking up right . . . NOW!

Nothing happens. The ANGEL spreads her wings. The room

becomes red hot. The ANGEL *extends her hands towards* HANNAH. HANNAH *walks towards her, and kneels. The* ANGEL *kisses her on the forehead and then the lips, a long, hot kiss.*

ANGEL. The Body is the Garden of the Soul.

HANNAH *has an enormous orgasm, as the* ANGEL *flies away to the accompanying glissando of a baroque piccolo trumpet.*

Scene Two

PRIOR WALTER *is in Heaven. He is dressed in prophet robes reminiscent of Charlton Heston's Moses drag in* The Ten Commandments. PRIOR *is carrying the Book of the Anti-Migratory Epistle. Heaven looks mostly like San Francisco after the Great 1906 Quake. It has a deserted, derelict feel to it, rubble is strewn everywhere. Seated on a wooden crate on a street corner is* HARPER, *playing with a cat.*

HARPER. Oh! It's you! My imaginary friend.

PRIOR. What are you doing here? Are you dead?

HARPER. No, I just had sex, I'm not dead! Why? Where are we?

PRIOR. Heaven.

HARPER. Heaven? I'm in Heaven?

PRIOR. That cat! That's Little Sheba!

HARPER. She was wandering around. Everyone here wanders. Or they sit on crates, playing card games. Heaven. Holy moly.

PRIOR. How did Sheba die?

HARPER. Rat poison, hit by a truck, fight with an alley cat, cancer, another truck, old age, fell in the East River, heartworms and one last truck.

PRIOR. Then it's true? Cats really have nine lives?

HARPER. That was a joke. I don't know how she died, I don't talk to cats I'm not that crazy. Just upset. We had sex, and then he . . . had to go. I drank an enormous glass of water and two Valiums. Or six. Maybe I overdosed, like Marilyn Monroe.

PRIOR. She didn't OD, she was assassinated by Jimmy Hoffa and JFK.

HARPER. Threshold of revelation?

PRIOR (*shaking his head no*). The Phil Donahue Show.

HARPER. Did you die?

PRIOR. No, I'm here on business.

HARPER. What kind of business?

PRIOR. I have to choose. I can return to the world. If I want to.

HARPER. Do you?

PRIOR. I don't know.

HARPER. I know. Heaven is depressing, full of dead people and all, but life.
    It's all a matter of the opposable thumb and forefinger; not of the hand but of the heart; we grab hold like nobody's business and then we don't seem to be able to let go.

PRIOR. To face loss. With grace. Is key, I think, but it's impossible. All you ever do is lose, and lose . . .

HARPER. But not letting go deforms you so.

PRIOR. The world's too hard. Stay here. With me.

HARPER. I can't. I feel like shit but I've never felt more alive. I've finally found the secret of all that Mormon energy. Devastation. That's what makes people migrate, build things. Heartbroken people do it, people who have lost love. Because I don't think God loves His people any better than Joe loved me. The string was cut, and off they went.
    I have to go now. I'm ready to lose him. Armed with the truth. He's got a sweet hollow centre, but he's the nothing man.
    I hope you come back. *Look* at this place. Can you imagine spending eternity here?

PRIOR. It's supposed to look like San Francisco.

HARPER (*looking around*). Ugh.

PRIOR. Oh but the real San Francisco, on earth, is unspeakably beautiful.

HARPER. Unspeakable beauty.
    That's something I would like to see.

HARPER *and* SHEBA *vanish.*

PRIOR. Oh! She . . . She took the cat. Come back, you took the . . .

Little pause.

Goodbye little Sheba. Goodbye.

The scenery dissolves and is replaced by an interior. A great antechamber to the Hall of the Upper Orders. It looks remarkably like the San Francisco City Hall, with much cracked plaster. The ANGEL *is there.*

ANGEL. Greetings, Prophet. We have been waiting for you.

Scene Three

Two a.m.. ROY's hospital room. ROY's body is on the bed. ETHEL is sitting in a chair. BELIZE enters, then calls off in a whisper.

BELIZE. Hurry.

LOUIS *enters wearing an overcoat and dark sunglasses.*

LOUIS. Oh my god, oh my god it's – Oh this is too weird for words, it's Roy Cohn, it's . . . so *creepy* here, I hate hospitals, I . . .

BELIZE. *Stop whining.* We have to move fast, I'm supposed to call the duty nurse if his condition changes and . . . (*He looks at* ROY.) It's changed.
    Take off those glasses you look ridiculous.

LOUIS *takes off the glasses. He has two black eyes, one cut.*

BELIZE. What happened to *you*? (*He touches the swelling near* LOUIS's *eye.*)

LOUIS. OW OW! (*He waves* BELIZE's *hand away.*) Expiation. For my sins. What am I doing here?

BELIZE. Expiation for your sins. I can't take the stuff out myself, I have to tell them he's dead and fill out all the forms, and I don't want them confiscating the medicine. I needed a pack-mule, so I called you .

LOUIS. Why me? You hate me.

BELIZE. I needed a Jew. You were the first to come to mind.

LOUIS. What do you mean you needed . . .

BELIZE. We're going to thank him. For the pills.

LOUIS. *Thank him?*

BELIZE. What do you call the Jewish prayer for the dead?

LOUIS. The Kaddish?

BELIZE. That's the one. Hit it.

LOUIS. Whoah, hold on.

BELIZE. Do it, do it, they'll be in here to check and he . . .

LOUIS. I'm not saying any fucking Kaddish for him. The drugs OK, sure, fine, but no fucking way am I praying for *him*. My New Deal Pinko Parents in Schenectady would never forgive me, they're already so disappointed, 'He's a fag. He's an office temp. And *now look*, he's saying Kaddish for Roy Cohn.' I can't believe you'd actually pray for . . .

BELIZE. Louis, I'd even pray for you.
    He was a terrible person. He died a hard death. So maybe . . . A queen can forgive her vanquished foe. It isn't easy, it doesn't count if it's easy, it's the hardest thing. Forgiveness. Which is maybe where love and justice finally meet. Peace, at least. Isn't that what the Kaddish asks for?

LOUIS. Oh it's Hebrew who knows what it's asking?

Little pause. LOUIS *looks at* ROY, *staring at him unflinchingly for the first time.*

LOUIS. I'm thirty-two years old and I've never been in a room with a dead body before. (*He touches* ROY's *forehead.*) It's so heavy, and small. I know probably less of the Kaddish than you do, Belize, I'm an intensely secular Jew, I didn't even Bar Mitzvah.

BELIZE. Do the best you can.

LOUIS *puts a Kleenex on his head.*

LOUIS. Yisgadal ve'yiskadash sh'mey rabo, sh'mey de kidshoh, uh . . . Boray pre hagoffen. No, that's the Kiddush, not the . . . Um, shema Yisroel adonai . . . . This is silly, Belize, I can't . . .

ETHEL (*standing, softly*). B'olmo deevro chiroosey ve'yamlich malchusey . . .

LOUIS. B'olmo deevro chiroosey ve'yamlich malchusey . . .

ETHEL. Bechayeychon uv'yomechechon uvchayey d'chol beys Yisroel . . .

LOUIS. Bechayeychon uv'yomechechon uvchayey d'chol beys Yisroel . . .

ETHEL. Ba'agolo uvizman koriv . . .

LOUIS. Ve'imroo omain.

ETHEL. Yehey sh'mey rabo m'vorach . . .

LOUIS and ETHEL. L'olam ulolmey olmayoh. Yisborach ve'yishtabach ve'yispoar ve'yisroman ve'yisnasey ve'yis'hadar ve'yisalleh ve'yishallol sh'mey dekudsho . . .

ETHEL. Berich hoo le'eylo min kol birchoso veshiroso . . .

LOUIS and ETHEL. Tushbchoso venechemoso, daameeron
  b'olmo ve'imroo omain. Y'he sh'lomo rabbo min sh'mayo
  v'chayim olenu v'al kol Yisroel, v'imru omain . . .

ETHEL. Oseh sholom bimromov, hu ya-aseh sholom olenu v'al
  col Yisroel . . .

LOUIS. Oseh sholom bimromov, hu ya-aseh sholom olenu v'al col
  Yisroel . . .

ETHEL. V'imru omain.

LOUIS. V'imru omain.

ETHEL. You sonofabitch.

LOUIS. You sonofabitch.

  ETHEL *vanishes*.

BELIZE. Thank you Louis, you did fine.

LOUIS. Fine? What are you talking about, fine? That was fucking
  miraculous.

Scene Four

Two a.m. JOE *enters the empty Brooklyn apartment, carrying the
suitcase from* LOUIS'*s.*

JOE. I'm back. Harper?

  He switches on a light.

  Harper?

  ROY *enters from the bedroom, dressed in a fabulous floor-
  length black velvet robe de chambre.* JOE *starts with terror,
  turns away, then looks again.* ROY'*s still there.*

JOE. What are you doing here?

ROY. Dead Joe doesn't matter.

JOE. No, no, you're not here, you . . .
    You lied to me. You said cancer, you said . . .

ROY. You could have read it in the papers. AIDS. I didn't want
  you to get the wrong impression.
    You feel bad that you beat somebody.

JOE. I want you to . . .

ROY. He deserved it.

JOE. No he didn't he . . .

ROY. Everybody does. Everybody could use a good beating.

JOE. I *hurt* him. I didn't . . . mean to, I didn't want to but . . .
I made him bleed. And he won't . . . ever see me again,
I won't . . .
   Louis.

He starts to cry.

   Oh God, please go, Roy, you're really frightening me, please
   please go.
      Harper.

ROY. Show me a little of what you've learned, baby Joe. Out in
the world.

   ROY *kisses* JOE *softly on the mouth.*

ROY. Damn.
   I gotta shuffle off this mortal coil. I hope they have
something for me to do in the Great Hereafter, I get bored easy.
   You'll find, my friend, that what you love will take you
places you never dreamed you'd go.

   ROY *vanishes.* HARPER *enters.* JOE *and* HARPER *stare at
each other.*

HARPER. Hope you didn't worry.

JOE. Harper?
   Where . . . Were you . . .

HARPER. A trip to the moon on gossamer wings.

JOE. What?

HARPER. You ought to get your hearing checked, you say that a lot.
   I was out. With a friend. In Paradise.

Scene Five

*Heaven: in the Council Room of the Continental Principalities. As
the scene is being set, a Voice (the same one heard in Act One
Scene One and Act Three Scene Three) proclaims:*

VOICE. In the Hall Of The Continental Principalities; Heaven, A
   City Much Like San Francisco. Six of Seven Myriad Infinite
   Aggregate Angelic Entities In Attendance, May Their Glorious

Names Be Praised Forever and Ever, Hallelujah. Permanent
Emergency Council is now in Session.

*The Continental Principalities sit around a table covered with
a heavy tapestry on which is woven an ancient map of the
world. The tabletop is covered with antique and broken
astronomical, astrological, mathematical and nautical objects
of measurement and calculation; heaps and heaps and heaps of
books and files and bundles of yellowing newspapers; inkpots,
clay tablets, styli and quill pens. The great chamber is dimly lit
by candles and a single great bulb overhead, the light of which
pulses to the audible rhythmic surgings and waverings of an
unseen generator. At the centre of the table is a single bulky
radio, a 1940s model in very poor repair. It is switched on and
glowing, and the ANGELS are gathered about it, intent upon
its dim, crackly signal.*

RADIO (*in a British accent*). . . . one week following the
explosion at the number four reactor, the fires are still burning
and an estimated . . . (*Static.*) . . . the disaster at the Chernobyl
Power Plant in Belarus is already by leagues the greatest
nuclear catastrophe in postwar . . . (*Static.*) . . . releasing into
the atmosphere fifty million curies of radioactive iodine,
six million curies of caesium and strontium rising in a plume
over five miles high, carried by the winds over an area
stretching from the Urals to thousands of miles beyond Soviet
borders, it . . . (*Static*) . . .

ASIATICA. We are losing the signal.

The ANGELS make mystic gestures. The signal returns.

RADIO. . . . falling like toxic snow into the Dnieper River,
which provides drinking water for thirty-five million Russians.
Radioactive debris contaminating over three hundred
thousand hectares of topsoil for a minimum of thirty years,
and . . . (*Static.*) . . . now hearing of thousands of workers who
have absorbed fifty times the lethal dose of . . . (*Static.*) . . .
BBC Radio, reporting live from Chernobyl, on the eighth day
of the . . .

The signal is engulfed in white noise and fades out.

ANTARCTICA. When?

OCEANIA. April 26th. Sixty-two days from today.

AFRICANII. How will they respond to this?

EUROPA. Die horribly. In multitudes.

OCEANIA. And then build more.

EUROPA. And die. In multitudes.

ANTARCTICA (*quietly*). I I I will rejoice to see it.

AUSTRALIA (*a polite but firm reprimand*). That. Is forbidden us.

ANTARCTICA. By Whom?

Some of the angels cough, some make mystic signs.

ASIATICA. This radio is a terrible radio.

AFRICANII. The reception is too weak.

EUROPA. A vacuum tube is blown.

OCEANIA. Dead.

AUSTRALIA. Can it be fixed?

EUROPA. That is Beyond Us.

AFRICANII. Actually it is a simple diode. Within are an anode and a cathode. The positive electrons travel from the cathode across voltage fields . . .

ASIATICA. Diodes are the product of the selfsame antinomic, divided human consciousness which produced the multifarious catastrophes of which We are impotent witness, dichotomous, propulsive . . .

OCEANIA (*overlapping on 'witness'*). The cathode, in fact, is negatively charged.

AFRICANII. No, positive. The anode is . . .

EUROPA. This device ought never to have been brought here. It is an Abomination, it is a Pandemonium, it is . . . .

OCEANIA. And without it, Oh Most Glorious Intelligences, How would we maintain surveillance over Human Mischief? With this? (*He brandishes an astrolabe.*)

EUROPA. I I I do not want to survey, it is beneath us, these anthill excursions, and between this crippled gadget and the mephitic plumes of that human-conceived Diabolus, that *reactor*, there is not a scintilla of difference . . .

AFRICANII (*overlapping on 'anthill'*). The positive electrons travel through a . . . They *are* negative, you are correct, I I I . . .

ANTARCTICA (*overlapping on 'reactor'*). I I I I do not weep for them, I I I weep for the vexation of the Blank Spaces, I weep for the Dancing Light, for the irremediable wastage of Fossil-Fuels, Old Blood of the Globe spilled wantonly or burned and jettisoned into the Crystal Air, I I I I delight in their suffering, I I I I will never relent, let them reap the harvest of . . .

AUSTRALIA (*overlapping on* AFRICANII'*s 'positive electrons'*).

If only He would Return I I I I do not know whether We have
Erred in transporting these dubious Things but . . . If We refer
to His Codex of Procedure, I I I cannot recall which page it was
on, but He has surely provided for the Conundrum . . .

ASIATICA (*overlapping on* EUROPA's *'diabolus'*). TRUE!
TRUE! Cathode Rays were discovered in America following
Einstein's publication of the Photo-electric Effect, and so
Einstein is the Thread of Presumption and accursed Invention
which unites these insidious interventions in the curved web of
Time and Distance which so disturbs . . .

EUROPA. Actually, it was Hayes, a European, who discovered the
cathode ray, and the patent was stolen by an American who
merely altered a few minor technical aspects of an inspiration
which was *MINE*, and . . .

AFRICANII. Regardless of the charge, it is the absence of resistance in a vacuum which . . .

OCEANIA (*overlapping on* ANTARCTICA's *'delight in their
suffering'*). And yet you *will* weep for them, Oh Heavens,
Be amazed, be appalled, be warned, for IN THAT DAY there
will be more than vexation on *earth* . . .

There is an enormous peal of thunder and a blaze of lightning.
PRIOR *and the* ANGEL OF AMERICA *are in the chamber,
standing before the council table. The Principalities stare at*
PRIOR.

ANGEL. Most August Fellow Principalities, Angels Most High:
I regret my absence at this session, I was detained.

Pause.

AUSTRALIA. Ah, this is . . . ?

ANGEL. The Prophet. Yes.

AUSTRALIA. Ah.

The ANGELS *bow.*

EUROPA. We were working.

AFRICANII. Making Progress.

Thunderclap.

PRIOR. I . . . I want to return this.

He holds out the Book. No one takes it from him.

AUSTRALIA. What is the matter with it?

PRIOR (*a beat, then*). It just . . . It just . . . We can't just stop.
We're not rocks, progress, migration, motion is . . . modernity.

It's *animate*, it's what living things do. We desire. Even if all
we desire is stillness, it's still desire *for*. Even if we go faster
than we should. We can't *wait*. And wait for what? God . . .

Thunderclap.

God . . .

Thunderclap.

He isn't coming back.
    And even if he did . . .
    If He ever did come back, if He ever *dared* to show His face,
or his Glyph or whatever in the Garden again . . . if after all this
destruction, if after all the terrible days of this terrible century
He returned to see . . . how much suffering His abandonment
had created, if He did come back you should *sue* the bastard.
That's my only contribution to all this Theology. Sue the
bastard for walking out. How dare He.

Pause.

ANGEL. Thus spake the prophet.

PRIOR (*starting to put the Book on the table*). So thank you . . .
for sharing this with me, but I don't want to keep it.

OCEANIA (*to the* ANGEL OF AMERICA). He wants to live.

PRIOR. Yes.
    I'm thirty years old, for Godsake.

Softer rumble of thunder.

I haven't done anything yet, I . . .
    I want to be healthy again. And this plague, it should stop.
In me and everywhere. Make it go away.

AUSTRALIA. Oh We have tried.
    We suffer with You but
    We do not know. We
    Do not know how.

PRIOR *and* AUSTRALIA *look at each other*.

EUROPA. This is the Tome of Immobility, of respite, of cessation.
    Drink of its bitter water once, Prophet, and never thirst
      again.

PRIOR. I . . . can't.

PRIOR *puts the Book on the table. He removes his prophet
robes, revealing the hospital gown underneath. He places the
robe by the Book.*

I still want . . . My blessing. Even sick. I want to be alive.

ANGEL. You only think you do.

> Life is a habit with you.
> You have not *seen* what is to come:
> We *have:*
> What will the grim Unfolding of these Latter Days bring?
> That you or any Being should wish to endure them?
> Death more plenteous than all Heaven has tears to mourn it,
> The slow dissolving of the Great Design,
> The spiralling apart of the Work of Eternity,
> The World and its beautiful particle logic
> All collapsed. All dead, forever,
> In starless, moonlorn onyx night.
> We are failing, failing,
> The Earth and the Angels.

The generator begins to fail, the lights to dim.

> Look up, look up,
> It is Not-to-Be Time.
> Oh who asks of the Orders Blessing
> With Apocalypse Descending?
> Who demands: More Life?
> When Death like a Protector
> Blinds our eyes, shielding from tender nerve
> More horror than can be borne.
> Let any Being on whom Fortune smiles
> Creep away to Death
> Before that last dreadful daybreak
> When all your ravaging returns to you
> With the rising, scorching, unrelenting Sun:
> When morning blisters crimson
> And bears all life away,
> A tidal wave of Protean Fire
> That curls around the planet
> And bares the Earth clean as bone.

Pause.

PRIOR. But still. Still.

> Bless me anyway.
>
> I want more life. I can't help myself. I do.
>
> I've lived through such terrible times, and there are people who live through much much worse, but . . . You see them living anyway.
>
> When they're more spirit than body, more sores than skin, when they're burned and in agony, when flies lay eggs in the corners of the eyes of their children, they live. Death usually has to *take* life away. I don't know if that's just the animal. I don't know if it's not braver to die. But I recognize the habit. The addiction to being alive. We live past hope. If I can find

hope anywhere, that's it, that's the best I can do. It's so much not enough, so inadequate but . . . Bless me anyway. I want more life.

PRIOR *begins to exit. The* ANGELS, *unseen by him, make a mystical sign. He turns again to face them.*

PRIOR. And if He returns, take Him to Court. He walked out on us. He ought to pay.

Scene Six

On the streets of Heaven. RABBI ISIDOR CHEMELWITZ *and* SARAH IRONSON *are seated on wooden crates with another crate between them. They are playing cards.*

PRIOR *enters.*

PRIOR. Excuse me, I'm looking for a way out of this, do you . . . Oh! You're . . .

SARAH IRONSON (*to the* RABBI). Vos vil er? [What does he want?]

RABBI ISIDOR CHEMELWITZ. Di Goyim, zey veysn nisht vi zikh oyftsufirn. [These Gentiles, they have no manners.]

PRIOR. Are you Sarah Ironson?

She looks up at him.

I was at your funeral! You look just like your grandson, Louis. I know him. Louis. He never wanted you to find out, but did you know he's gay?

SARAH IRONSON (*not understanding*). Vi? [What?]

RABBI ISIDOR CHEMELWITZ. Dein aynickl, Louis? [Your grandson, Louis?]

SARAH IRONSON. Yeah?

RABBI ISIDOR CHEMELWITZ (*sotto voce*). Er iz a feygele. [He is a fag.]

SARAH IRONSON. A *feygele*? Oy.

RABBI ISIDOR CHEMELWITZ. Itst gistu. [You deal.]

PRIOR. Why does everyone here play cards?

RABBI ISIDOR CHEMELWITZ. Why? (*To Sarah.*) Dos goy vil visn far-Vos mir shpiln in kortn. [The goy wants to know why

we play cards.]
    OK.
    Cards is strategy but mostly a game of chance. In Heaven,
everything is known. To the Great Questions are lying about
here like yesterday's newspaper all the answers. So from what
comes the pleasures of Paradise? *Indeterminacy!* Because
mister, with the Angels, those makhers, may their names be
always worshipped and adored, it's all gloom and doom and
give up already. But still is there Accident, in this pack of
playing cards, still is there the Unknown, the Future. You
understand me? It ain't all so much mechanical as they think.
    You got another question?

PRIOR. I want to go home.

RABBI ISIDOR CHEMELWITZ. Oh simple. Here. To do this,
    every Kabbalist on earth would sell his right nut.
        Penuel, Peniel, Ja'akov Beth-Yisroel, Killeeyou, killeemee,
    OOO-oooooooo-OOOO-oooooohmayn!

The ladder, the music and the lights. PRIOR *starts to descend.*

SARAH IRONSON. Hey! Zogt Loubeleh az di Bobbe zogt.

RABBI ISIDOR CHEMELWITZ. She says tell this Louis
    Grandma says:

SARAH IRONSON. Er iz tomid geven a bissele farblonjet, shoin
    vi a boytshikl. Ober siz nisht keyn antshuldigunk.

RABBI ISIDOR CHEMELWITZ. From when he was a boy he
    was always mixed up. But it's no excuse.

SARAH IRONSON. *He should have visited!* But I forgive. Tell
    him: az er darf ringen mit zain Libm nomen. Yah?!

RABBI ISIDOR CHEMELWITZ. You should struggle with the
    Almighty!

SARAH IRONSON. Azoi toot a Yid.

RABBI ISIDOR CHEMELWITZ. It's the Jewish way.

Scene Seven

As PRIOR *journeys to earth he sees* ROY, *at a great distance, in
Heaven, or Hell, or Purgatory – standing waist deep in a
smouldering pit, facing a great flaming Aleph, which bathes him
and the whole theatre in a volcanic, pulsating red light.
Underneath, a basso profundo roar, like a thousand Bessemer*

furnaces going at once, deep underground.

ROY. Paternity suit? Abandonment? Family court is my particular
metier, I'm an absolute fucking demon with Family Law. Just
tell me who the judge is, and what kind of jewellery does he
like? If it's a jury, it's harder, juries take more talk but
sometimes it's worth it, going jury, for what it saves you in
bribes. Yes I will represent you, King of the Universe, yes I
will sing and eviscerate, I will bully and seduce, I will win for
you and make the plaintiffs, those traitors, wish they had never
heard the name of . . .

Huge thunderclap.

Is it a done deal, are we on? Good, then I gotta start by telling
you you ain't got a case here, you're guilty as hell, no question,
you have nothing to plead but not to worry, darling, I will make
something up.

Scene Eight

It's morning, the next day. PRIOR *descends from Heaven and slips
into bed.* BELIZE *is sleeping in a chair.*

PRIOR (*waking*). Oh.
I'm exhausted.

BELIZE (*waking*). You've been working hard.

PRIOR. I feel terrible.

BELIZE. Welcome back to the world.

PRIOR. From where, I . . . Oh. Oh I . . .

EMILY *enters.*

EMILY. Well look at this. It's the dawn of man.

BELIZE. Venus rising from the sea.

PRIOR. I'm wet.

EMILY. Fever broke. That's a good sign, they'll be in to change
you in . . .

PRIOR (*looking around*). Mrs. Pitt? Did she . . .

BELIZE. Elle fait sa toilette. Elle est *très* formidable, ça. Where
did you find her?

PRIOR. We found each other, she . . .
     I've had a remarkable dream. And you were there, and
you . . .

     HANNAH *enters*.

PRIOR. And you.

HANNAH. I what?

PRIOR. And some of it was terrible, and some of it was
     wonderful, but all the same I kept saying I want to go home.
     And they sent me home.

HANNAH (*to* PRIOR). What are you talking about?

PRIOR (*to* HANNAH). Thank you.

HANNAH. I just slept in the chair.

PRIOR (*to* BELIZE). She saved my life.

HANNAH. I did no such thing, I slept in the chair. Being in
     hospital upsets me, it reminds me of things.
     I have to go home now. I had the most *peculiar* dream.

     There's a knock on the door. It opens. LOUIS *enters*.

LOUIS. Can I come in?

     Brief tense pause; PRIOR *looks at* LOUIS *and then at*
     BELIZE.

EMILY. I have to start rounds.

     (*To* PRIOR.) You're one of the lucky ones. I could give you a
     rose. You rest your weary bones.

PRIOR (*to* LOUIS). What are you . . .

     He sees LOUIS's *cuts and bruises*.

     What happened to *you*?

LOUIS. Visible scars. You said . . .

PRIOR. Oh Louis, you're so goddamned literal about everything.

HANNAH. I'm going now.

PRIOR. You'll come back.

HANNAH (*a beat, then*). If I can. I have things to take care of.

PRIOR. Please do.
     I have always depended on the kindness of strangers.

HANNAH. Well that's a stupid thing to do. (*Exits*.)

LOUIS. Who's she?

PRIOR (*a beat, then*). You really don't want to know.

BELIZE. Before I depart. A homecoming gift.

> BELIZE *puts his shoulder bag in* PRIOR's *lap.* PRIOR *opens it; it's full of bottles of pills.*

PRIOR (*squinting hard*). What? I can't read the label, I . . .
> My eyes. Aren't any better.
> (*Squints even harder.*) AZT?
> Where on earth did you . . . These are hot pills. I am shocked.

BELIZE. A contribution to the get-well fund. From a bad fairy.

LOUIS. These pills, they . . . they make you better.

PRIOR. They're poison, they make you anaemic.
> This is my life, from now on, Louis. I'm not getting 'better'.
> (*To* BELIZE.) I'm not sure I'm ready to do that to my bone marrow.

BELIZE (*taking the bag*). We can talk about it tomorrow. I'm going home to nurse my grudges. Ta, baby, sleep all day. Ta, Louis, you sure know how to clear a room. (*He exits.*)

LOUIS. Prior.
> I want to come back to you.

Scene Nine

Same morning. Split scene: LOUIS *and* PRIOR *in* PRIOR's *hospital room, as before;* HARPER *and* JOE *in Brooklyn, as at the end of Act Five Scene Four.*

HARPER. I want your credit card.
> That's all. You can keep track of me from where the charges come from. If you want to keep track. I don't care.

JOE. I have some things to tell you.

HARPER. Oh we shouldn't talk. I don't want to do that anymore.
> Credit card.

JOE. I don't know what will happen to me without you. Only you.
> Only you love me. Out of everyone in the world. I have done things, I'm ashamed. But I have changed. I don't know how yet, but . . .
> Please, please, don't leave me now.
> Harper.
> You're my good heart.

She looks at him, she walks up to him and slaps him, hard.

HARPER (*quietly*). Did that hurt?

   JOE *nods yes.*

HARPER. Yes. Remember that. Please.
   If I can get a job, or something, I'll cut the card to pieces.
   And there won't be charges anymore. Credit card.

JOE takes out his wallet, gives her his card.

JOE (*small voice, not looking at her*). Call or . . . Call. You have
   to.

HARPER. No. Probably never again. That's how bad.
   Sometimes, maybe lost is best. Get lost. Joe. Go exploring.

*She digs in the sofa. She removes her Valium stash. She shakes
out two pills, goes to JOE, takes his hand and puts the Valium
in his open palm.*

With a big glass of water. (*She leaves.*)

LOUIS. I want to come back to you.
   You could . . . respond, you could say something, throw me
   out or say it's fine, or it's not fine but sure what the hell or . . .

Little pause.

I really failed you. But . . . this is hard. Failing in love isn't the
same as not loving. It doesn't let you off the hook, it doesn't
mean . . . you're free to not love.

PRIOR. I love you Louis.

LOUIS. Good. I love you.

PRIOR. I really do.
   But you can't come back. Not ever.
   I'm sorry. But you can't.

Scene Ten

*That night. LOUIS and PRIOR remain from the previous scene.
JOE is sitting alone in Brooklyn. HARPER appears. She is in a
window seat on board a jumbo jet, airborne.*

HARPER. Night flight to San Francisco. Chase the moon across
   America.
      God! It's been years since I was on a plane!
      When we hit thirty-five thousand feet, we'll have reached

the tropopause. The great belt of calm air. As close as I'll ever get to the ozone.

I dreamed we were there. The plane leapt the tropopause, the safe air and attained the outer rim, the ozone, which was ragged and torn, patches of it threadbare as old cheesecloth, and that was frightening . . .

But I saw something only I could see, because of my astonishing ability to see such things:

Souls were rising, from the earth far below, souls of the dead, of people who had perished, from famine, from war, from the plague, and they floated up, like skydivers in reverse, limbs all akimbo, wheeling and spinning. And the souls of these departed joined hands, clasped ankles, and formed a web, a great net of souls, and the souls were three-atom oxygen molecules, of the stuff of ozone, and the outer rim absorbed them, and was repaired.

Nothing's lost forever. In this world, there is a kind of painful progress. Longing for what we've left behind, and dreaming ahead.

At least I think that's so.

EPILOGUE: Bethesda   February 1990

PRIOR, LOUIS, BELIZE *and* HANNAH *sitting on the rim of the Bethesda Fountain in Central Park. It's a bright day, but cold. PRIOR is heavily bundled, and he has thick glasses on and supports himself with a cane. HANNAH is noticeably different – she looks like a New Yorker, and she is reading the* New York Times. LOUIS *and* BELIZE *are arguing. The Bethesda* ANGEL *is above them all.*

LOUIS. The Berlin Wall has fallen. The Ceausescus are out. He's building democratic socialism. The New Internationalism. Gorbachev is the greatest political thinker since Lenin.

BELIZE. I don't think we know enough yet to start canonizing him. The Russians hate his guts.

LOUIS. Yeah but. Remember back four years ago? The whole time we were feeling everything everywhere was stuck, while in Russia! Look! Perestroika! The Thaw! It's the end of the cold war! The whole world is changing! Overnight!

HANNAH. I wonder what'll happen now in places like Czechoslovakia and Yugoslavia.

LOUIS. Yugoslavia?

PRIOR (*to audience*). Let's just turn the volume down on this, OK?
They'll be at it for hours. It's not that what they're saying isn't important, it's just . . .
This is my favourite place in New York City. No, in the whole universe. The parts of it I have seen.
On a day like today. A sunny winter's day, warm and cold at once. The sky's a little hazy, so the sunlight has a physical presence, a character. In autumn, those trees across the lake are yellow, and the sun strikes those most brilliantly. Against the blue of the sky, that sad fall blue, those trees are more light than vegetation. They are Yankee trees, New England transplants. They're barren now.
It's January 1990. I've been living with AIDS for five years. That's six whole months longer than I lived with Louis.

LOUIS. Whatever comes, what you have to admire in Gorbachev, in the Russians is that they're making a leap into the unknown. You can't wait around for a theory. The sprawl of life, the weird . . .

HANNAH. Interconnectedness . . .

LOUIS. Yes.

BELIZE. Maybe the sheer size of the terrain.

LOUIS. It's all too much to be encompassed by a single theory now.

BELIZE. The world is faster than the mind.

LOUIS. That's what politics is. The world moving ahead. And only in politics does the miraculous occur.

BELIZE. But that's a theory.

HANNAH. You need an idea of the world to go out into the world. But it's the going into that makes the idea. You can't wait for a theory, but you have to have a theory.

LOUIS. As my grandma said, go know.

PRIOR. This angel. She's my favourite angel.
    I like them best when they're statuary. They commemorate death but they suggest a world without dying. They are made of the heaviest things on earth, stone and iron, they weigh tons but they're winged, they are engines and instruments of flight.
    This is the angel Bethesda. Louis will tell you her story.

LOUIS. Oh. Um, well, she was this angel, she landed in the Temple square in Jerusalem, in the days of the Second Temple, right in the middle of a working day she descended and just her foot touched earth. And where it did, a fountain shot up from the ground. When the Romans destroyed the Temple, the fountain of Bethesda ran dry.

PRIOR. And Belize will tell you about the nature of the fountain, before its flowing stopped.

BELIZE. If anyone who was suffering, in the body or the spirit, walked through the waters of the fountain of Bethesda, they would be healed, washed clean of pain.

PRIOR. They know this because I've told them, many times. Hannah here told it to me. She also told me this:

HANNAH. When the Millennium comes . . .

PRIOR. Not the year two thousand, but the Capital M Millennium . . .

HANNAH. Right. The fountain of Bethesda will flow again. And I told him I would personally take him there to bathe. We will all bathe ourselves clean.

LOUIS. Not literally in Jerusalem, I mean we don't want this to have sort of Zionist implications.

BELIZE. Right on.

LOUIS. But on the other hand we *do* recognize the right of the state of Israel to exist.

BELIZE. But the West Bank should be a homeland for the Palestinians and the Gaza Strip . . .

LOUIS. Well not *both* the Gaza Strip and the West Bank, I mean no one supports Palestinian rights more than I do but . . .

BELIZE Oh yeah right, Louis, like not even the Palestinians are more devoted than . . .

PRIOR. I'm almost done.
    The fountain's not flowing now, they turn it off in the winter, ice in the pipes. But in the summer it's a sight to see. I want to be around to see it. I plan to be. I hope to be.
    This disease will be the end of many of us, but not nearly all, and the dead will be commemorated and will struggle on with the living, and we are not going away. We won't die secret deaths anymore. The world only spins forward. We will be citizens. The time has come.
    Bye now.
    You are fabulous creatures, each and every one.
    And I bless you: *More Life*.
    The Great Work Begins.

The End